Heart of Darkness

Joseph Conrad (originally Józef Teodor Konrad Korzeniowski) was born in the Ukraine in 1857 and grew up under Tsarist autocracy. His parents, ardent Polish patriots, died when he was a child, following their exile for anti-Russian activities, and he came under the protection of his tradition-conscious uncle, Tadeusz Bobrowski, who watched over him for the next twenty-five years. In 1874 Bobrowski conceded to his nephew's passionate desire to go to sea, and Conrad travelled to Marseilles, where he served in French merchant vessels before joining a British ship in 1878. In 1886 he obtained British nationality and his Master's certificate in the British Merchant Service. Eight years later he left the sea to devote himself to writing, publishing his first novel, *Almayer's Folly*, in 1895. The following year he married Jessie George and eventually settled in Kent, where he produced within fifteen years such modern classics as *Youth*, *Heart of Darkness*, *Lord Jim*, *Typhoon*, *Nostromo*, *The Secret Agent* and *Under Western Eyes*. He continued to write until his death in 1924. Today Conrad is generally regarded as one of the greatest writers of fiction in English – his third language. He once described himself as being concerned 'with the ideal value of things, events and people'; in the Preface to *The Nigger of the 'Narcissus'* he defined his task as 'by the power of the written word . . . before all, to make you *see*'.

Robert Hampson is a Reader in English at Royal Holloway, University of London. He is the author of *Joseph Conrad: Betrayal and Identity* (1992) and *Writing Malaysia: Cross-Cultural Encounters in Conrad's Malay Fiction* (2000). He is a former editor of the journal, *The Conradian*, for the Joseph Conrad Society (UK). For Penguin he has also edited Conrad's *Victory* and Kipling's *Something of Myself* and co-edited Conrad's *Lord Jim*.

JOSEPH CONRAD

Heart of Darkness

with

The Congo Diary

Edited with an Introduction and Notes by
ROBERT HAMPSON

PENGUIN BOOKS

PENGUIN BOOKS

Published by the Penguin Group
Penguin Books Ltd, 80 Strand, London WC2R 0RL, England
Penguin Putnam Inc., 375 Hudson Street, New York, New York 10014, USA
Penguin Books Australia Ltd, 250 Camberwell Road, Camberwell, Victoria 3124, Australia
Penguin Books Canada Ltd, 10 Alcorn Avenue, Toronto, Ontario, Canada M4V 3B2
Penguin Books India (P) Ltd, 11 Community Centre, Panchsheel Park, New Delhi – 110 017, India
Penguin Books (NZ) Ltd, Cnr Rosedale and Airborne Roads, Albany, Auckland, New Zealand
Penguin Books (South Africa) (Pty) Ltd, 24 Sturdee Avenue, Rosebank 2196, South Africa

Penguin Books Ltd, Registered Offices: 80 Strand, London WC2R 0RL, England

www.penguin.com

This edition first published 1995
Reprinted in Penguin Classics 2000

14

Introduction and Notes copyright © Robert Hampson, 1995
he Congo Diary from Last Essays by Joseph Conrad copyright Doubleday, a division of
Bantam Doubleday Dell Publishing Group Inc., 1926, and appears by permission of
Doubleday, a division of Bantam Doubleday Dell Publishing Group Inc.
All rights reserved

The moral right of the editor has been asserted

Set in 10.5/13.5 pt Monotype Ehrhardt
Set by Datix International Limited, Bungay, Suffolk
Printed in England by Clays Ltd, St Ives plc

CONTENTS

ACKNOWLEDGEMENTS

In preparing this edition, I am indebted to the work of numerous Conradians. I owe particular debts to Norman Sherry's *Conrad's Western World* (Cambridge: Cambridge University Press, 1971) and to earlier editors: Cedric Watts (ed.), *Heart of Darkness and Other Tales* (Oxford: The World's Classics, 1990); Robert Kimbrough (ed.), *Heart of Darkness* (New York: W.W. Norton & Co., 1988); Zdzisław Najder (ed.), *Congo Diary and Other Uncollected Pieces* (Garden City, New York: Doubleday & Company, 1978); Józef Miłobędzki (ed.), 'Joseph Conrad's *Congo Diary*', *Nautologia*, 1 (1972). I am grateful to the Beinecke Library, Yale University, for allowing me to see the manuscript of *Heart of Darkness*; to the Houghton Library, Harvard University, for allowing me to see Conrad's *Congo Diary*; to the Henry W. and Albert A. Berg Collection, the New York Public Library, for allowing me to examine the typescript of *Heart of Darkness*; and to the Rosenbach Foundation, Philadelphia, for allowing me to examine corrected page proofs. In addition, I am grateful to the librarians at Royal Holloway, University of London; at the University of London Library; at the British Library; and at the National Maritime Museum, Greenwich, for their assistance. Felix Driver, June Hampson, Owen Knowles, Andrew Michael Roberts, Bhaskar Sengupta and David Thomason have provided information, stimulation, and support at different stages in the research. I owe a particular debt to Hans van

ACKNOWLEDGEMENTS

Marle for his comments on the Introduction and Notes and for his assistance, of various sorts, with *The Congo Diary*. Finally, I am grateful to Royal Holloway, University of London, for the period of sabbatical leave that allowed me to complete my work on this edition.

INTRODUCTION

1 Books and Maps

In October 1874 the sixteen-year-old Józef Teodor Konrad Korzeniowski left Kraków by train for Marseilles. Within two months he had started the sea-life that was to provide the novelist Joseph Conrad with so much of the material for his early fiction: on 15 December 1874 he sailed out of Marseilles as a passenger on board the *Mont-Blanc*, bound for Martinique; six months later, on 25 June 1875, he repeated the same voyage, but this time as an apprentice. Marseilles remained his base for almost three years until April 1878, when a new phase of his existence started with his sailing in the British steamer *Mavis*. A career in French ships was closed to him because of changes in the regulations relating to the employment of foreigners in the French merchant navy, and he began now the association with the British Merchant Marine that was to last until January 1894, when he signed off in London as the second mate of the *Adowa*. Although he tried for a number of other ships subsequently, his sea-life had ended and a new career as a writer was about to begin.

In later life Conrad offered various explanations for his desire to go to sea. In *A Personal Record* he raised the question: '. . . why should I, the son of a land which such men as these have turned up with their ploughshares and bedewed with their blood, undertake the pursuit of fantastic meals of salt junk and hard tack upon the wide seas?'[1] His answer was that his imagination had been captured by his boyhood reading of such books as Victor Hugo's *Travailleurs de la mer* (*Toilers of the Sea*), which he described as 'my first introduction to the sea in literature' (*PR*, p. 72). Conrad's essay 'Tales of the Sea' had already described the sea novels of James Fenimore Cooper and Captain Frederick Marryat as having 'shaped' his life.[2] *A Personal Record* suggests another kind of reading that had also captured his imagination:

It was in 1868, when nine years old or thereabouts, that while looking at a map of Africa of the time and putting my finger on the blank space then representing the unsolved mystery of that continent, I said to myself with absolute assurance and an amazing audacity which are no longer in my character now:

'When I grow up I shall go *there*.'

And of course I thought no more about it till after a quarter of a century or so an opportunity offered to go there ... I did go there: *there* being the region of Stanley Falls which in '68 was the blankest of blank spaces on the earth's figured surface. (*PR*, p. 13)

In *Heart of Darkness* Conrad gives Marlow a similar boyhood experience:

'[. . .] Now when I was a little chap I had a passion for maps. I would look for hours at South America, or Africa, or Australia, and lose myself in all the glories of exploration. At that time there were many blank spaces on the earth, and when I saw one that looked particularly inviting on a map (but they all look that) I would put my finger on it and say, When I grow up I will go there. The North Pole was one of these places, I remember. Well, I haven't been there yet, and shall not try now. The glamour's off. Other places were scattered about the Equator, and in every sort of latitude all over the two hemispheres. [. . .] But there was one yet – the biggest, the most blank, so to speak –

that I had a hankering after.

'True, by this time it was not a blank space any more. It had got filled since my boyhood with rivers and lakes and names. It had ceased to be a blank space of delightful mystery – a white patch for a boy to dream gloriously over. It had become a place of darkness. [. . .]' (*HD*, pp. 21–2)[3]

Marlow's career, like Conrad's, spans a significant period in the history of relations between Europe and Africa: when Conrad was a boy in the 1860s and 1870s, much of Africa remained unknown to Europeans; when he actually went to Africa as a man, he participated in what had become the 'scramble' for Africa. Notice also the change that has taken place on the map: 'the blankest of blank spaces' has acquired 'rivers and lakes and names', but also, more surprisingly, from being 'a white patch for a boy to dream gloriously over', it has become 'a place of darkness'. Christopher L. Miller notes that the passage doesn't actually identify 'Africa' as 'the biggest, the most blank' space on the map; that 'Africa' is not mentioned subsequently in the novel; and suggests that 'the reader – teased into thinking he is reading a book "about" Africa' is actually 'led into a void that . . . has no name but "heart of darkness"'.[4] Certainly, where the scientific/positivist project seeks to replace the unknown with the known, Marlow's narrative in *Heart of Darkness* begins by suggesting that exploration has turned a blank space into a space of darkness and ends by suggesting that it has turned the unknown into the 'unspeakable'. Indeed, one might argue that, instead of bringing light into darkness as it claims, the 'civilizing' mission actually uncovers the 'darkness' at its own heart. As V.G. Kiernan puts it, Africa in this period 'became very truly a Dark Continent, but its darkness was one the invaders brought with them, the sombre shadow of the white man'.[5]

II Geography and Some Explorers

The tidal current runs to and fro in its unceasing service, crowded with memories of men and ships it has borne to the rest of home or to the battles of the sea. It had known and served all the men of whom the nation is proud, from Sir Francis Drake to Sir John Franklin, knights all, titled and untitled – the great knights-errant of the sea. It had borne all the ships whose names are like jewels flashing in the night of time, from the *Golden Hind* returning with her round flanks full of treasure, to be visited by the Queen's Highness [. . .] to the *Erebus* and *Terror*, bound on other conquests – and that never returned. (*HD*, p. 17)

Before I consider *Heart of Darkness*, it is worth looking at some aspects of the late-Victorian context in which it was produced. In his late essay 'Geography and Some Explorers', Conrad returned again to his childhood fascination with the map of Africa, and to the way in which, at that time, 'the dull imaginary wonders of the dark ages' had been replaced by 'exciting spaces of white paper': 'My imagination could depict to itself there worthy, adventurous and devoted men, nibbling at the edges, attacking from north and south and east and west, conquering a bit of truth here and a bit of truth there, and sometimes swallowed up by the mystery their hearts were so persistently set on unveiling.'[6] For the last time in print, Conrad returned to childhood memories of the map of Africa:

I stand here confessed as a contemporary of the Great Lakes. Yes, I could have heard of their discovery in my cradle, and it was only right that, grown to a boy's estate, I should have in the later 'sixties done my first bit of map-drawing and paid my first homage to the prestige of their first explorers. It consisted in entering laboriously in pencil the outline of Tanganyika on my beloved old atlas, which, having been published in 1852, knew nothing, of course, of the Great Lakes. The heart of its Africa was white and big. (*LE*, p. 20)

Then he records once again how he put his 'finger on a spot in the very middle of the then white heart of Africa' and 'declared that some day [he] would go there': 'Nothing was further from my wildest hopes. Yet it is a fact that, about eighteen years afterwards, a wretched little stern-wheel steamboat I commanded lay moored to the bank of an African river' (*LE*, p. 24).

'Geography and Some Explorers' traces the development of geography from its 'fabulous phase' (*LE*, p. 4) through the phase of what Conrad calls 'geography militant'. The 'fabulous phase', a phase of 'circumstantially extravagant speculation', includes the fantastic visions of medieval cartography, which 'crowded its maps with pictures of strange pageants, strange trees, strange beasts' (*LE*, p. 3). 'Geography militant', to which most of Conrad's essay is devoted, has two different aspects. On the one hand, exploration was 'prompted by an acquisitive spirit, the idea of lucre in some form, the desire of trade or the desire of loot, disguised in more or less fine words' (*LE*, p. 14). On the other hand, 'geography militant' gave birth to scientific geography, where the 'only object was the search for truth', and the explorers 'devoted themselves to the discovery of facts in the configuration and features of the main continents' (*LE*, p. 14). In his account of this development Conrad is very conscious of what he calls 'the drama of human endeavour' (*LE*, p. 2): whether it is the Conquistadores' adventures in the New World, 'those pertinacious searchers for El Dorado who climbed mountains, pushed through forests, swam rivers, floundered in bogs, without giving a single thought to the science of geography' (*LE*, p. 5), who characterize the acquisitive aspect of 'militant geography', or various

African explorers, Mungo Park in the Sudan, Bruce in Abyssinia, Burton and Speke around the Great Lakes, and, above all, David Livingstone in Central Africa, 'the most venerated, perhaps, of all the objects of my early geographical enthusiasm' (*LE*, p. 24), who exemplify scientific geography.

The scientific aspect of 'militant geography' is also represented for Conrad by the Polar explorers, and here, as Conrad puts it, the 'dominating figure' (*LE*, p. 15) is Sir John Franklin. In May 1845 Franklin sailed from Greenhithe with two ships, the *Erebus* and the *Terror*, with provisions for three years, on what turned out to be a successful quest for the North-West Passage. It also turned out to be his last expedition. The two ships were sighted, on 28 July 1845, in Baffin's Bay, and then no more was seen or heard from them. From 1848 onwards successive attempts were made to find him and his men: Captain Ommanney's 1850 voyage found traces of the expedition; Dr Rae's 1854 expedition heard from the Inuits about their sighting, four years earlier, of a group of white men dragging a boat along the west shore of King William's Island (and the subsequent discovery of their bodies at the mouth of the Great Fish River); in 1857 Captain McClintock's expedition conclusively established the fate of Franklin and his men. In his book about his search for Franklin, *The Voyage of the 'Fox' in the Arctic Seas*, McClintock notes that, when Franklin's expedition sailed into Arctic waters, 'the charts ... were little more than sheets of blank paper'.[7] A note dated 1847, which the McClintock expedition found at the northern end of King William's Land where the expedition had wintered for 1846/7, said simply 'All Well'.[8] At this point they had sailed over five hundred miles of previously unexplored waters and were within ninety miles of the known sea off the coast of North America. But Franklin died that June, and the following spring the *Erebus* and *Terror* were still stuck in the ice. They had been stuck there for over a year and a half, and they had supplies that would last only until July. On 22 April 1848 the two ships were abandoned. According to McClintock's reconstruction of events, the survivors attempted to retreat to the Hudson Bay territories up the Great Fish River (*VF*, p. 247), but they all died from a combination of disease, cold and starvation. Towards the end of his book McClintock observes: 'that amongst all the relics of the ill-fated expedition no preserved meat or vegetable tins were found, either about the cairns or along the line of retreat; the inference is as plain as it is painful' (*VF*, p. 299). McClintock's oblique allusion supports Dr Rae's report that the last survivors had resorted to cannibalism in an attempt to save their lives.[9] Perhaps this is what Conrad had in mind, when he referred to the expedition as 'the darkest drama perhaps played behind the curtain of Arctic mystery' (*LE*, p. 15).

In this essay, 'Geography and Some Explorers', Conrad dwells at some length on McClintock's account of his expedition to find Franklin. Not only did he read McClintock's book as a boy, but he has read it 'many times since' and even now has on his shelves 'a copy of a popular edition' (*LE*, p. 16).[10] McClintock's narrative of the voyage of the *Fox* in search of Franklin conveys succinctly the excitements and dangers of the quest and also the peculiarities of the harsh Arctic environment, an area so sparsely populated and so inhospitable that the traces of earlier expeditions are still visible. The first major discovery that McClintock reports was the large boat from the Franklin expedition that was found on the shore east of Cape Crozier. The markings on the side, once deciphered, indicated that it had passed through Woolwich Dockyard: 'built by contract, numbered 61, and received into Woolwich Dockyard in April 184—, the fourth figure to the right hand was lost' (*VF*, p. 250). The boat contained portions of two human skeletons, fragments of clothing, and five or six small books, including a small bible with marginal, handwritten annotations. This chimes with (and perhaps anticipates) Marlow's 'extraordinary find' on his way up-river to find Kurtz, the book he finds in the abandoned hut:

Its title was, 'An Inquiry into some Points of Seamanship,' by a man Tower, Towson – some such name – Master in his Majesty's Navy [. . .] Such a book being there was wonderful enough; but still more astounding were the notes pencilled in the margin, and plainly referring to the text. (*HD*, pp. 65–6)

Andrea White has noted that Conrad 'was influenced from an early age by the legends about and writings by the heroic figure of the day, the explorer–adventurer'.[11] *The Voyage of the 'Fox' in the Arctic Seas* is clearly an important intertext for *Heart of Darkness*, but another is a book written by an explorer who is *not* mentioned in 'Geography and Some Explorers', namely *In Darkest Africa* (1890) by Henry Morton Stanley.

III Stanley and Leopold

'[. . .] Sometimes he was contemptibly childish. He desired to have kings meet him at railway-stations on his return from some ghastly Nowhere, where he intended to accomplish great things. [. . .] (*HD*, p. 110)

In May 1873 David Livingstone, the celebrated missionary–explorer, died at Ilala in the heart of Africa. For Livingstone, Commerce, Christianity and Civilization would work together as the counter to the slave-trade, which was still growing throughout the area of his wanderings in Africa, with Zanzibar under its Arab ruler and the Portuguese possessions as the main centres. One of Conrad's memories in 'Geography and Some Explorers' hints at this trade:

Everything was dark under the stars. Every other white man on board was asleep. I was glad to be alone on deck, smoking the pipe of peace after an anxious day. The subdued thundering mutter of the Stanley Falls hung in the heavy night air of the last navigable reach of the upper Congo, while no more than ten miles away, in Reshid's Camp just above the Falls, the yet unbroken power of the Congo Arabs slumbered uneasily. (*LE*, pp. 24–5)

Reshid was the nephew of the notorious slave-trader Hamid Ibn Muhammad, known as Tippu Tib. Perhaps Conrad is silent about Arab slavery in *Heart of Darkness* because of the way in which the 'war against slavery' in Africa was so often used to justify colonial expansion. Alternatively, perhaps he omitted references to it in order to emphasize Marlow's sense of 'an empty stream, a great silence, an impenetrable forest' (*HD*, p. 59). The fiction accentuates the isolation of the white man and the 'mysteriousness' of the Africans to reproduce the paradigm of the heroic explorer as exemplified in the popular narrative of the meeting of Stanley and Livingstone.

Stanley, who had 'found' Livingstone on Lake Tanganyika in November 1871, returned to Europe the following year in a blaze of publicity. As Felix Driver has noted, the journalist-turned-explorer Stanley was not only an adept self-publicist – with *How I Found Livingstone* (1872), *Through the Dark Continent* (1878), *The Congo and the Founding of Its Free State* (1885) and *In Darkest Africa* – but he was also the subject of public controversy:

The first and most celebrated of these controversies occurred during the summer of 1872, when Stanley returned from his search for Livingstone; the second erupted in 1876, when reports of violence on

Stanley's second African expedition reached London; and the third developed in 1890–91, in the wake of Stanley's mission to 'rescue' Emin Pasha, the German Governor of Equatorial Sudan.[12]

The 1872 controversies came from three sources: rival newspapers, personal friends of the British Agent at Zanzibar (whom Stanley had criticized) and the Royal Geographical Society. The dispute between Stanley and the Royal Geographical Society turned on 'issues of social standing, scientific merit and moral legitimacy' (Driver, p. 147), but the dispute also turned on what was felt to be Stanley's attempt to appropriate Livingstone's reputation: Stanley had not only found Livingstone but also, like Marlow with Kurtz, he had been entrusted with Livingstone's private journals and letters.[13]

In April 1874 Livingstone's body finally reached England to receive a hero's funeral in Westminster Abbey with Stanley as one of the pall-bearers. Later that year Stanley returned to Africa. He travelled to Zanzibar on an expedition, commissioned by the *New York Herald* and co-sponsored by the *Daily Telegraph*, that would take him across Africa to Boma. The 1876 controversy was sparked off by Stanley's newspaper account of a violent incident at Bambireh Island on Lake Victoria.[14] In 1875 Stanley had fallen foul of the inhabitants of the island: they had refused him food, threatened him with spears and arrows, pulled his hair and stolen the oars from his boat, the *Lady Alice*, named after his 'Intended', Alice Pike. Subsequently, Stanley had returned to Bambireh with a force of 280 men and, having enticed the inhabitants on to the shore, fired round after round of bullets into them. It was not just the fact that he used force that stirred up the controversy, but the ruthless nature of the force and the apparent enjoyment of that ruthlessness in his account of the incident. As the *Saturday Review* observed: 'He has no concern with justice, no right to administer it; he comes with no sanction, no authority, no jurisdiction – nothing but explosive bullets and a copy of the *Daily Telegraph*.'[15]

This issue was reopened by the Royal Geographical Society on Stanley's return to England in 1878. The controversy this time ranged around the gulf between Stanley's claims of high moral purpose and his method of 'exploration by warfare': he had written in his diary about his hope to succeed Livingstone 'in opening up Africa to the shining light of Christianity', but in *Through the Dark Continent* he had argued that Africans respect only 'force, power, boldness and decision'.[16] A joint committee of the Anti-Slavery and Aborigines Protection Societies complained in the *Colonial Intelligencer*: 'the murderous acts of retaliation he committed were unworthy of a man who went to Africa professedly as a pioneer of civilization'.[17]

However, if Stanley met criticism in England, he received a very different response from Belgium. In his journey to England, he had been met, on 8 January 1878, by secret emissaries from King Leopold at Marseilles Railway Station. Two years earlier Leopold had been impressed by a report on 'African Exploration' in *The Times*, which described a country of 'unspeakable riches' just waiting for 'an enterprising capitalist' to 'take the matter in hand'.[18] Leopold had had an interest in colonialism since the 1850s. As Neal Ascherson puts it, colonialism, for Leopold, meant 'the very limited science' of using technologically less-developed populations 'to produce wealth from the natural resources of their own country'.[19] Leopold had also realized that 'forced labour' was an even cheaper mode of production than paid labour. Six months after reading the article on 'African Exploration', in September 1876, he had organized the first geographical conference on Central Africa, the Conférence Géographique Africaine, to which various celebrated explorers were invited. At the conference he announced his moral crusade: 'To open to civilization the only part of our globe where it has yet to penetrate, to pierce the darkness which envelops whole populations, it is a crusade worthy of this century of progress.'[20] In June 1878 Stanley had accepted Leopold's invitation to go to Brussels. By the autumn he had agreed to serve Leopold in Africa for a term of five years: the 'philanthropical and scientific' mission was to open up Africa under the auspices of the International Association (Association Internationale pour l'Exploration et la Civilisation en Afrique) through a series of 'stations' and by constructing a road between Boma and Stanley Pool; the covert plan, as Stanley quickly realized, was to make the Congo basin a Belgian colony.

Stanley's last expedition (1887–90) had, as its ostensible purpose, the relief of Emin Pasha (then apparently under threat from the Mahdist movement). For political reasons, however, the expedition to the Sudan was routed through the Congo. Leopold had given Stanley two diplomatic tasks: the first, which he achieved, was to persuade the slave-dealer Tippu Tib to become Governor of Stanley Falls (since the Congo state had not enough money to afford a war with the Arabs, who were competing for control of Central Africa); the second, which he failed to achieve, was to persuade Emin Pasha to bring his province, Equatoria, into the Congo Free State. The first stage of the journey took Stanley and his forces up the Congo from the mouth to Matadi – the journey that Conrad and Marlow were to make a few years later. The narrative of *In Darkest Africa* begins with a tension between the urgent need to reach Emin Pasha ('Emin will be lost unless immediate aid be given him') and the delays occasioned by the absence of river-worthy steamers for the Upper Congo.[21] Stanley observes: 'The whole of the naval stock promised did not exist at all except in the imagination of the gentleman of the Bureau at Brussels' (*DA*, p. 50). The steamers were 'wrecked, rotten, or without boilers or engines' (*DA*, p. 50), and Stanley describes the repairs, the replacement of plates and so on, that were necessary before the expedition could get under way again. Both these motifs – the urgent need to reach someone up-river and delays occasioned by the need to repair a steamer – were also to become part of Marlow's experience. It is perhaps worth noting that Emin Pasha was a rank and not a name: the man Stanley's expedition was trying to reach was Eduard Schnitzler, whom Stanley described as 'a great linguist, Turkish, Arabic, German, French, Italian and English being familiar to him' (*DA*, p. 40). We might also notice that, even in Stanley's own account, the expedition was organized not just to rescue Emin Pasha, nor even to explore the area between the Congo and Equatorial Sudan. Stanley remarks, in *In Darkest Africa*, that 'Emin Pasha possessed about seventy-five tons of ivory. So much ivory would amount to £60,000' (*DA*, p. 42), and he made arrangements not only to bring back the ivory but also to distribute the £60,000.

On his return Stanley was given a hero's welcome in Brussels and in London. On 19 April 1890 Stanley's party were met at the French frontier by a special train sent by Leopold, which was met at the Gare du Midi by a guard of honour, and on 26 April he was met by similar cheering crowds in London at Charing Cross Station.[22] Conrad, meanwhile, had had an interview in Brussels in February 1890 and, after a ten-week stay in Poland, was back in Brussels by 29 April to hear the confirmation of his three-year appointment to the Congo.

In addition to his work for Leopold, Stanley was not slow to associate his missions with the advancement of various material interests – the Belgians in the Congo, the British in East Africa and the Sudan, and even the Americans in Zanzibar. As Driver observes: 'The sheer variety of the political claims on

Stanley suggests that he did not represent the interests of any empire in particular: he was instead a pioneer of the new imperialism in general' (Driver, pp. 165–6). Driver compares him to Kurtz ('"all Europe contributed" to his making'); but equally one might ask Marlow's question, 'How many powers of darkness claimed him for their own?' (*HD*, p. 81)

IV In Darkest Africa

As Norman Sherry has pointed out, when Conrad went up the Congo in May 1890, it would have been difficult for him not to have been aware of Stanley. Conrad arrived back in Marseilles on 15 February 1878 – just over a month after Stanley's arrival there *en route* for England after finding Livingstone. In January 1889 Stanley's message that he had found Emin Pasha reached London, and, as a result, 'throughout that summer further news of his expedition continued to be published in the press'.[23] In November of that year Conrad's boyhood ambition to go to Africa reasserted itself, and he went to Brussels to be interviewed by Albert Thys of the Société Anonyme Belge pour le Commerce du Haut-Congo.[24] Conrad was in Brussels in February 1890, during which he formed a close relationship with his cousin's widow, Marguerite Poradowska (whom he referred to as his 'aunt'), and again at the end of April and early in May. On 10 May 1890 he left Bordeaux in the *Ville de Maceio* for the Congo. On 12 June he disembarked at Boma, the seat of government, and next day journeyed to Matadi, where he was delayed for over a fortnight. As his diary notes, he left Matadi on 28 June by overland route for Kinshasa, the Central Station of *Heart of Darkness*, which he reached on 2 August.[25] In his journey from the mouth of the Congo, Conrad must have been conscious of following in Stanley's footsteps: for example, the missionary, Mr Bentley, whom he records failing to meet, was the missionary from whom Stanley had forcibly requisitioned the *Peace* to transport the Emin Pasha expedition up the Congo.

On 13 August, Conrad left Kinshasa for the 1,000-mile trip to Stanley Falls in the *Roi des Belges*.[26] The passage quoted earlier from 'Geography and Some Explorers' offered a glimpse of Conrad at Stanley Falls 'smoking the pipe of peace after an anxious day'. The state of Conrad's mind is revealed by the continuation: he did not feel a sense of excitement or achievement; instead, 'a great melancholy descended' on him as he realized that 'the idealised realities of a boy's daydreams' had been displaced and befouled by the activities of Stanley and the Congo Free State, or, as he put it, by 'the unholy recollection of a prosaic newspaper "stunt" and the distasteful knowledge of the vilest scramble for loot that ever disfigured the history of human conscience and geographical exploration' (*LE*, p. 25).

After the captain of the *Roi des Belges* fell sick, Conrad took over command for part of the return journey, arriving back in Kinshasa on 24 September. A sick company agent, Georges Antoine Klein, was taken on board the steamer and died during the course of this journey.[27] The next three months were occupied by Conrad's own illness, convalescence and a slow, six-week journey to the coast: he reached Matadi on 4 December and soon after sailed from Boma back to Europe. The first half of 1891 was taken up with illness and convalescence, and then, during the summer, he made two trips along the Thames estuary in the yawl the *Nellie*. The *Nellie* belonged to his friend, G.F.W. Hope, a former 'Conway boy' who was now a company director, and they were accompanied by W.B. Keen, an accountant, and T.L. Mears, a lawyer.

In December 1898 Conrad began work on *Heart of*

Darkness.[28] In his 'Author's Note' he describes the tale as 'experience pushed a little (and only very little) beyond the actual facts of the case'. Some of the changes between the manuscript and the published text suggest the narrative's basis in Conrad's personal experience, but also, by their excision, one way in which Conrad moves the tale away from autobiography. For example, the sea-journey to the mouth of the Congo originally began 'I left in a French steamer and beginning with Dakar she called in every blamed port they have out there' and ended 'we passed various places: Gran' Bassam, Little Popo, names that seemed to belong to some sordid farce'. But he cut 'beginning with Dakar' and he inserted 'with names like' before 'Gran' Bassam'. The effect, in both cases, is to weaken the connection with Conrad's own experience and to move away from African specificities. As Miller notes, 'the only African place-names left in *Heart of Darkness* after Marlow's description of the "blank space" are thus transformed from fact to simile, from places with names to places with names "like" these' (*BD*, p. 175). The tale promises not an 'image of Africa' but a self-conscious exploration of imagings of Africa, the language and tropes of a cross-cultural encounter.[29]

Another way in which Conrad tried to push 'beyond the actual facts of the case' was by augmenting the details of his own journey up and down the Congo with other narratives of exploration. McClintock's quest for Franklin and Stanley's quest for Emin Pasha were only two of the intertexts in Conrad's development of the narrative he created around the dying agent Klein.[30] The adventure narrative is disrupted and overwritten with a range of discourse types and a variety of literary and mythical patterns. Marlow's physical journey from London to the Congo becomes a moral journey in which he confronts the workings of colonialism and a psychological journey undertaken by Marlow, his audience and the reader, while his story-telling draws upon the resources of a literary culture that includes Homer, Virgil, Dante, Bunyan and Goethe in his attempt to represent and comprehend the non-European experience. 'All Europe contributed to the making of Kurtz' and 'all Europe' contributes to Marlow's narrative. His narrative can be read as a quest; a *katabasis*; an inverted pilgrim's progress; while Kurtz's experience suggests a version of the Faustian pact.[31]

Perhaps the most important way in which Conrad distances himself from his material is through his use of Marlow. *Heart of Darkness* not only has two narrators (Marlow and the anonymous first narrator who introduces him) but the inter-action between Marlow and his audience means that Marlow's utterances are provided with a context while the utterances of the anonymous narrator are as much the product of a specific viewpoint as Marlow's. There is clearly a displacement between Conrad and the anonymous narrator, so that Marlow is doubly displaced from Conrad. The basic narrative structure of *Heart of Darkness* is a frame-tale with inset stories. Conrad had experimented with this method of 'oblique narration', the tale within a tale, in 'Youth', which has a similar narrative situation: 'a director of companies, an accountant, a lawyer', and an unnamed narrator gathered together for a tale by Marlow.[32] One development from 'Youth' is that, where framed tale and frame-tale in 'Youth' set up alternate visions, that of the youthful, romantic Marlow and that of the jaded middle-aged Marlow, the relationship between the two in *Heart of Darkness* is more complex: a web of parallels and contrasts produces what Cedric Watts has called 'a tentacular effect' (Watts, p. 26), in which apparent contrasts often turn out to be parallels. As Daphna Erdinast-Vulcan observes: 'the ostensi-bly clear-cut distinction between the two narratives is consist-ently probed'.[33] Consider, for example, the 'bones' that the accountant 'toys' with on board the *Nellie* or the grand piano in the Intended's drawing-room: both connect the fetish of ivory at the heart of darkness with the civilized world of Marlow's audience in a net of complicity. This is part of a narrative strategy that sets up antitheses only to break them down again, that erases the boundaries between self and other even as Marlow struggles to maintain them, in order to question the reader's positioning of themselves in relation to the narrative. Another development is that Marlow's story is not primarily about himself. The thrust of the narrative is towards Kurtz and Kurtz's experience – initially focused on how to evaluate Kurtz (as 'devil' or 'angel'), it comes to focus on Kurtz as a 'voice' and potential explainer of Marlow's experience. The centre it points towards is Kurtz's story. After the first section Kurtz becomes the focus of interest, and the repeated references to Kurtz's 'eloquence' contain the implicit promise that Kurtz, with his 'gift' of 'expression', will articulate the secret and provide the solution to the moral, psychological and philosophical problems that the journey has presented, but there is a deliberate anti-climax in relation to Kurtz that expresses the story's radical scepticism about ultimate values and about the possibility of explanation.

Ian Watt has suggested that '*Heart of Darkness* embodies more thoroughly than any previous fiction the posture of uncertainty and doubt.'[34] Not only does it use oblique narration to produce an open-ended fiction, but epistemological doubts are expressed through the device which Watt has called 'delayed decoding'.[35] The narrative presents the character's immediate sensations ('Something big appeared in the air before the shutter, the rifle went overboard, and the man stepped back swiftly [. . .]' *HD*, p. 77), only to open up a gap between impression and interpretation and to foreground the process of interpretation.[36] Peter Brooks has similarly explored

Heart of Darkness's uncertainties from a narratological perspective.[37] Where the classic framed tale produces a set of nested boxes, of brackets within brackets, Marlow's narrative plot steadily takes as its story what Marlow understands to be Kurtz's story, but Kurtz's story 'never fully exists, never fully gets itself told' (Brooks, p. 252). Marlow's journey back to origins promises to gain its meaning from its attachment to Kurtz's prior journey, but Kurtz's articulation at what Marlow identifies as 'the farthest point of navigation and the culminating point of my experience' (*HD*, p. 21) is 'a blurted emotional reaction of uncertain reference and context' which 'makes a mockery of story-telling and ethics' (Brooks, p. 250). After Marlow has retraced Kurtz's journey up-river through the stories of other quests and journeys, Kurtz's own story is at last conveyed to Marlow in a non-narrated way, 'in desolate exclamations, completed by shrugs, in interrupted phrases, in hints ending in deep sighs' (*HD*, p. 93). It becomes one among a series of possible plots, of alternative signifying systems, that offer to explain reality 'if only one could believe them' (Brooks, p. 239). In the end Marlow's own narrative arrives only at the suggestion of a motive for its own telling: as if the conventional narrative ending he supplies in Brussels has condemned him to the guilty unconventional narration he produces on the Thames.

v The Idea of Empire

'[. . .] The conquest of the earth, which mostly means the taking it away from those who have a different complexion or slightly flatter noses than ourselves, is not a pretty thing when you look into it too much. What redeems it is the idea only. An idea at the back of it; not a sentimental pretence but an idea; and an unselfish belief in the idea

– something you can set up, and bow down before, and offer a sacrifice to. . . . [. . .]' (*HD*, p. 20)

Since he was writing *Heart of Darkness* for *Blackwood's Magazine*, Conrad had a fairly clear conception of the nature of his immediate readership: conservative and imperialist in politics, and predominantly male.[38] He wrote to William Blackwood, the publisher, in advance to reassure him: 'The title I am thinking of is "The Heart of Darkness" – but the narrative is not gloomy. The criminality of inefficiency and pure selfishness when tackling the civilising work in Africa is a justifiable idea.'[39] The first sentence suggests something of the reliability of Conrad's statements in this letter. The second sentence, with its criticism of inefficiency and its apparent endorsement of 'the civilising work in Africa', curiously echoes Marlow's preamble to the story of his own collusion with imperialism. Marlow describes the Roman colonization of Britain in terms that suggest an obvious parallel with later British imperialism, but he offers the disclaimer: 'Mind, none of us would feel exactly like this. What saves us is efficiency' (*HD*, p. 20). This utterance, like Conrad's statement to Blackwood, apparently remains within the frame of reference of imperialist discourse. However, when Marlow recounts his meeting with the Company's chief accountant at the Central Station, the moral inadequacy of 'efficiency' as a justification within a colonial context is clearly affirmed. After Marlow's praise of the chief accountant for 'keeping up his appearance' (his 'starched collars and got-up shirt-fronts were achievements of character'), Marlow's narrative reveals the dissociated sensibility that lies behind the accountant's efficient book-keeping:

'[. . .] When a truckle-bed with a sick man (some invalided agent from up-country) was put in there, he exhibited a gentle annoyance. "The groans of this sick person," he said, "distract my attention. And without that it is extremely difficult to guard against clerical errors in this climate." [. . .]' (*HD*, p. 37)[40]

In the opening section of *Heart of Darkness* Conrad deploys various strategies in relation to the implied reader, the conservative, white, male reader of *Blackwood's Magazine*. To begin with, there is the evocation of 'the great spirit of the past' (*HD*, p. 17) by the unnamed first narrator. This celebration of British trade and exploration 'from Sir Francis Drake to Sir John Franklin' constitutes what Joyce critics term a 'reader trap'.[41] Conrad offers, through this anonymous narrator, the kind of nationalist history and imperialist rhetoric with which his first readers would have been familiar in order to lull them into a false sense of security at the outset. However, for the careful or experienced reader, hints of a different vision are suggested towards the end: 'Hunters for gold or pursuers of fame, they had all gone out on that stream, bearing the sword, and *often* the torch, messengers of the *might* within the land [my italics]' (*HD*, p. 17). Just as the words used subtly subvert the narrator's confident rhetoric, the reference to Sir Francis Drake might also have reminded some of Conrad's first readers of a less than flattering article on Drake that had appeared in *Blackwood's* six months earlier, while the reference to Sir John Franklin's expedition arguably implants an allusion to European cannibalism at the start of the novella.[42] Marlow's affirmation of the 'idea' that redeems imperialism in his preamble is an even clearer example of a 'reader trap'. On a first reading it can lead the reader to assume that the story that follows is to be an exploration and enunciation of that 'idea'. It is only on subsequent readings that proper weight is given to the image with which Marlow concludes ('something you can set up, and bow down before, and offer a sacrifice to. . . .'), and that the reader begins to appreciate the psychological dynamics implicitly underlying both the aposiopesis with which the speech ends and Marlow's impulse to narrate the tale that follows. Marlow's assertion of the redeeming 'idea' behind imperialism leads him into figurative language which subverts the idea he has been asserting. Marlow's speech breaks off, and it breaks off because he realizes the implications of the image he has just used. Marlow, after all (according to the logic of realism), knows the end of the story he is about to tell, and the story concerns not (as the first-time reader might have been led to expect) the redeeming 'idea' behind imperialism but rather someone who, encouraged by the power-relations and discourse of imperialism, sets himself up as something for others to 'bow down before, and offer a sacrifice to. . . .'[43] Indeed, it might be argued that it is this image that prompts Marlow's story rather than any search to express the redeeming 'idea'. As in those *gestalt* drawings that can be read as either a vase or two profiles, as foreground and background change places, here language that is offered as figurative suddenly asserts its literal meaning, and this kind of unsettling of language proves to be a characteristic feature of Marlow's narration.[44]

VI An Image of Africa

'[. . .] Land in a swamp, march through the woods, and in some inland post feel the savagery, the utter savagery, had closed round him . . . [. . .]' (*HD*, p. 19)

Chinua Achebe's famous attack on *Heart of Darkness* refuses to consider either the text's dramatization of Marlow's consciousness or Conrad's strategic use of the distance between himself and his English narrators.[45] Conrad is not presenting an image of Africa but rather Marlow's experience of Africa and Marlow's attempt to understand and represent that experience. Marlow is a fictional character whose consciousness operates according to contemporary codes and categories. If Marlow's perceptions are at times racist, it is because those codes and conventions were racist. As Anthony Fothergill has pointed out, Marlow is 'conscious enough of some racial stereotypes to turn them ironically against their white users', but he is ultimately caught up in complicity and contradictions at a cultural and political level.[46] However, Conrad's narrative method (which Achebe dismisses) represents a more radical stance than Marlow's, since it objectifies and problematizes Marlow's narrative, his perceptions and representations.

The nub of Achebe's criticism of Conrad is the kind of reading of *Heart of Darkness* that sees it only in psychological terms: 'Can nobody see the preposterous and perverse arrogance in thus reducing Africa to the role of props for the break-up of one petty European mind?' As Achebe asserts, a psychological (or, indeed, metaphysical) reading that focuses only on Kurtz or Marlow and ignores the social and historical context replicates the dehumanization of Africans that *Heart of Darkness*'s critique of imperialism deplores. Achebe also argues that African culture and history have been denied adequate representation in European writing, and that *Heart of Darkness* does nothing to remedy this. Here W. Holman Bentley's *Pioneering on the Congo* (1900) provides an instructive comparison.[47] Bentley devotes the first two chapters of his two-volume account of the twenty years he spent as a missionary in the Congo to a history of the Congo from 1484 to 1877, and his narrative generally gives much more sense of social relations and social organization within and between different peoples in the Congo basin than *Heart of Darkness* does, but his history of the Congo is written from the perspective of European contact with the Congo and his narrative generally is firmly fixed within a racist and imperialist Christian framework. Edward Said has described Orientalism as more 'a sign of European-Atlantic power over the Orient' than 'a veridic discourse about the Orient', and that distinction is also important in relation to Africa.[48] If *Heart of Darkness* does not offer a representation of Africa, it foregrounds the power-relation between Europe and Africa and, through its staging of a narrator in a specific narrative situation, holds up for analysis the European discourses produced in that context. Said argues that:

The imaginative examination of things Oriental was based more or less exclusively upon a sovereign Western consciousness . . . according to a detailed logic governed not simply by empirical reality but by a battery of desires, repressions, investments, and projections.[49]

And it is precisely those 'desires, repressions, investments, and projections' that *Heart of Darkness* exposes in the discourses of imperialism. Africa is not the arbitrarily selected backdrop for a story about 'the break-up of one petty European mind': Kurtz's 'break-up' is the result of his place in the hierarchically structured engagement of Europe and Africa; Kurtz is a victim of one of the discourses of imperialism; and Kurtz's history shows how damaging that discourse is to both Africans and Europeans.

Achebe also ignores the implied reader of *Heart of Darkness*. As Benita Parry observes:

Conrad in his 'colonial fictions' did not presume to speak for the colonial peoples nor did he address them . . . His original constituents were the subscribers to *Blackwood's* . . . an audience still secure in the conviction that they were members of an invincible imperial power and a superior race.[50]

Conrad's position was similar to that faced by anthropologists when they return to their own country to write up their research: 'they must do so in the conventions of representation already circumscribed . . . by their discipline, institutional life, and wider society'.[51] Conrad shows his understanding of the parameters within which he was writing by mirroring them in Marlow's relations with his audience. Marlow's audience, like the readership of *Blackwood's Magazine*, is made up of males of the colonial service class. Marlow is forced to confront the problem of making his experience intelligible to an audience that readily manifests the limits of its understanding and tolerance: '"Try to be civil, Marlow," growled a voice' (*HD*, p. 60). Marlow adopts various rhetorical strategies in relation to this particular audience, and, as we have seen, Conrad similarly shapes his narrative strategies to a specific implied reader. But, far from purveying 'comforting myths' (as Achebe alleges), the narrative strategies of both Conrad and Marlow work to subvert many of the assumptions accepted by their audience.

One area where this clearly happens is in relation to imperialist discourse and its antithetical language of 'light' and 'darkness', 'civilized' and 'savage'. Sherry draws attention to a speech made by Stanley, which compared the Roman colonization of Britain with the British in Africa. It concluded: 'God forbid that we should any longer subject Africa to the same dreadful scourge and preclude the light of knowledge which has reached every other quarter of the globe from having access into her coasts.'[52] As Eric Woods has argued, light/darkness imagery in imperialist discourse contained an ambivalence that proved ideologically useful.[53] On the one hand, as this speech illustrates, it implies a moral imperative (to bring light into areas of darkness) and thus justified missions and settlements. On the other hand, it also served to consolidate fixed categories, a perception of 'us' and 'them'. By contrast Conrad's handling of this imagery breaks down this sense of fixed opposition and undermines the implied 'moral imperative'. After the first narrator evokes 'the great spirit of the past upon the lower reaches of the Thames' (*HD*, p. 17), Marlow responds to his images of light and darkness by observing 'And this also [. . .] has been one of the dark places of the earth' (*HD*, p. 18), Marlow then explains this statement by reference to the Roman colonization of Britain, where the 'savages' feared by the 'civilized man' are the natives of the Thames valley. The ascription of 'savagery' to the other is clearly a projection of the fears of the colonizer in an environment and among a people he cannot comprehend. By the end of the narrative, with the return to the Thames, a Thames that 'flowed sombre under an overcast sky', that 'seemed to lead into the heart of an immense darkness' (*HD*, p. 124), it is clear that 'darkness' is not something safely in the past ('nineteen hundred years ago'), nor is it something 'other'. Instead of affirming the opposition of darkness and light, civilized and savage, Marlow's narrative works to destabilize it: darkness is located at the heart of the 'civilizing' mission.

Yet, as Frances B. Singh suggests, there is a dislocation between the political and metaphysical aspects of the narrative.[54] While *Heart of Darkness* is clearly critical of colonization, and presents the Africans as the innocent victims of European greed and will-to-power, the imagery of darkness it uses as metaphysical discourse associates 'evil' with the categories used in anthropological descriptions of 'primitive' peoples. The narrative carries the implication that Kurtz's 'evil' is signalled by his 'going native', and that 'evil, in short, *is* African'.[55] While the narrative makes it clear that the will-to-power implicit in the very idea of a 'civilizing mission' is what leads Kurtz to set himself up as a god, the fact that he sets himself up as a tribal god reinstates the idea of racial superiority at a deeper level than the critique of colonialism.

VII A World of Their Own

'[. . .] It's queer how out of touch with truth women are. They live in a world of their own, and there had never been anything like it, and never can be. [. . .]' (*HD*, p. 28)

Peter Hyland has argued that Achebe's critique of the representation of Africans can also be extended to the representation of women, and *Heart of Darkness* has been criticized both for its demeaning, stereotypical representation of women and for its exclusion of the female reader.[56] Marlow's critical comments on his aunt and his idealization of the Intended reflect Victorian patriarchal stereotypes: in both cases what Marlow perceives is not the woman herself but an image based on his own preconceptions about women. A stereotype is asserted to avoid confronting the 'otherness' of women, and the sexual fear underlying this particular manoevre is even more evident in Marlow's representation of the African woman at the Inner Station: 'the colossal body of the fecund and mysterious life seemed to look at her, pensive, as though it had been looking at the image of its own tenebrous and passionate soul' (*HD*, p. 99). Johanna M. Smith has noted how the jungle's absorption of Kurtz is imaged as 'sexual cannibalism': 'it had taken him, loved him, embraced him, got into his veins, consumed his flesh' (*HD*, p. 81).[57] Through Marlow's conflation of woman and jungle, itself based on an ideological alignment of male/ female with culture/nature, the 'heart of darkness' can be read as Marlow's fear of women projected on to the jungle. The threat the African woman embodies is subsequently repressed by asserting the myth of the pure, self-sacrificing woman, the myth that Marlow imposes on the Intended, although that imposition is itself destabilized by the threatened return of the repressed. There is, as Hyland notes, 'a supreme irony, and a revelation of truth, surely unperceived by Marlow, in his substitution of "your name" for "The horror! The horror!"' (Hyland, pp. 9–10) in his conversation with the Intended. At the same time, as Jeremy Hawthorn notes, the juxtaposition of the two women repeats 'a familiar pattern': 'woman as devoted and chaste spirit, and woman as sensual and sexual flesh' (Hawthorn, p. 186), a patriarchal discourse that divides and dehumanizes women.

Though women are marginalized by Marlow's narration, they actually usher Marlow into the experience he recounts. It is Marlow's aunt who has the influence to get him a job when his own efforts have failed. At the start of Marlow's narrative is this disorienting experience, when his assumptions about power and gender are undermined, and Marlow's unease at the experience of his own powerlessness is recuperated through irony at the expense of his aunt and women in general. In the same way it is women who guard 'the door of Darkness' (*HD*, p. 26), and Marlow's uneasiness ('She seemed to know all about them and about me, too'), again related to women in positions of power and knowledge, is this time recuperated through literary distancing ('*Ave!* Old knitter of black wool. *Morituri te salutant.*') Women also, arguably, constitute the experience that Marlow recounts. As Hyland suggests, it is the 'wild and gorgeous apparition' of the African woman, rather than Kurtz, who is for Marlow 'the central enigma at the heart of darkness' (Hyland, p. 8). Certainly, it is the African woman and the Intended who are the focus of the final part of Marlow's narrative. If Kurtz sets himself up as a god to be worshipped, Marlow here sets up the Intended for his own ambivalent act of worship: as he 'bows down' before what he conceives of as the Intended's faith, 'that great and saving illusion' (*HD*, p.121), he simultaneously reasserts and imposes on her the patriarchal ideology of separate spheres, a female world of illusion ('too beautiful altogether') and a male world of truth ('too dark altogether'). Marlow's lie to the Intended shows how what presents itself as an act of venerating women actually asserts and protects men.

Nina Pelikan Straus has commented on the way in which Marlow 'presents a world distinctly split into male and female realms', and she probes how the female reader positions herself in relation to a text that operates in terms of the secret sharing of male characters at the expense of women and the circulation of discourse between men, a circle of communication that includes the implied reader and excludes the concerns of women.[58] For Straus, the 'guarding of secret knowledge' is 'the undisclosed theme of *Heart of Darkness*' (Straus, p. 134): Marlow's narrative and narration together imply that the 'truth' about Kurtz can be revealed only to those '"man" enough to take it', but, for Straus, *Heart of Darkness* reveals not so much 'the truth of our times' as 'a certain kind of male self-mystification whose time is passing if not past', an assertion of male heroism and plenitude which is predicated upon 'female cowardice and emptiness' (Straus, p. 135).

Conrad's staging of Marlow's narration of his journey towards the 'heart of darkness' has come a long way, then, from the careful note-taking of the anxious young Pole on his journey from Matadi to Kinshasa. Where Korzeniowski was concerned with the notation of time, distance, landscape, weather (and the state of his own health), Conrad's objectification of Marlow's narrative, his distanced representation of Marlow's representations, opens *Heart of Darkness* on to a critical reading of its range of late-Victorian discursive practices and creates the possibility for the reader of going beyond the narrator's conceptual and ideological limitations.

Notes

1. *A Personal Record* (London: J.M. Dent, 1923), p. 35; all subsequent references will be to this edition, cited in the text as *PR*. This series of reminiscences first appeared in Ford Madox Ford's *English Review* (December 1908–June 1909) and was subsequently published as a book under the title *Some Reminiscences* (London: Eveleigh Nash, 1912).

2. 'Perhaps no two authors of fiction influenced so many lives and gave to so many the initial impulse towards a glorious or a useful career', *Notes on Life and Letters* (London: J.M. Dent, 1924), p. 56. This essay first appeared in *Outlook* (4 June 1898) and was first collected in the volume *Notes on Life and Letters* (London: J.M. Dent, 1921).

3. For more about Arctic exploration, see the account of the Franklin expedition ('Introduction', pp. xiv–xv). This perhaps explains why Marlow feels that 'the glamour's off'.

4. Christopher L. Miller, *Blank Darkness: Africanist Discourse in French* (Chicago: University of Chicago Press, 1985), pp. 173–4, hereafter cited as *BD*. In the same way, as Anthony Fothergill notes, *Heart of Darkness* avoids specificities of dates (*Heart of Darkness*, [Milton Keynes: Open University Press, 1989], pp. 24–5, hereafter cited as Fothergill).

5. V.G. Kiernan, *The Lords of Humankind: Black Man, Yellow Man, and White Man in an Age of Empire* (1969; London: Century Hutchinson, 1988), p. 226.

6. *Last Essays* (London: J.M. Dent, 1926), pp. 19–20, hereafter cited as *LE*. The essay was written as a general introduction to a serial publication called *Countries of the World* and appeared as 'The Romance of Travel' in the first number, February 1924. It was reprinted in the *National Geographic Magazine* (March 1924).

7. F. Leopold McClintock, *The Voyage of the 'Fox' in the Arctic Seas* (London: John Murray, 1859), p. 33; hereafter cited in the text as *VF*.

8. As Conrad observes in his essay, editions of McClintock's book contained 'the touching facsimile of the printed form filled in with a summary record of the two ships' work, the name of "Sir John Franklin

commanding the expedition" written in ink, and the pathetic underlined entry "All Well"' (*LE*, p. 16).

9. In articles in *Household Words* and the *London Illustrated News*, Rae had reported how 'from the mutilated state of many of the bodies' and the 'contents of the kettles' it was evident that some members of the expedition 'had been driven to the last dread alternative' to try to sustain life. David Woodman, in the most recent study of the expedition, *Unravelling the Franklin Mystery: Inuit Testimony* (Montreal: McGill-Queen's University Press, 1991), offers a convincing and radical reconstruction of events through the use of Inuit testimony, and provides further evidence of cannibalism.

10. Like A.R. Wallace's *Malay Archipelago*, which Conrad described as his 'favourite bedside book', *The Voyage of the 'Fox'* is one of those books from Conrad's library that left a mark on his fiction. See Richard Curle, 'Joseph Conrad: Ten Years Later', which records Conrad's general love for 'old memoirs and travels' as well as his particular love for Wallace's work (*Virginia Quarterly Review*, 10 [1934], p. 431).

11. Andrea White, *Joseph Conrad and the Adventure Tradition: Constructing and Deconstructing the Imperial Subject* (Cambridge: Cambridge University Press, 1993), p. 2.

12. Felix Driver, 'Henry Morton Stanley and His Critics: Geography, Exploration and Empire', *Past & Present*, 133 (November 1991), pp. 134–64, especially p. 136; hereafter cited as Driver. I am deeply indebted to this article for much of my account of Stanley.

13. Driver observes that Stanley 'lacked the credentials of a gentleman or a scientist' (p. 147); he was suspect as an American and as a journalist; also, under his adopted American status, it was discovered that he was concealing his origins as an illegitimate child from a Welsh workhouse.

14. *Daily Telegraph*, 7 and 10 August 1876.

15. *Saturday Review*, 16 February 1878; quoted in Driver, p. 151.

16. D. Stanley (ed.), *The Autobiography of Sir Henry Morton Stanley* (London, 1909), p. 295; Henry M. Stanley, *Through the Dark Continent* (London, 1878), I, p. 216.

17. Driver, p. 158. In this controversy Stanley was accused of excessive violence, wanton destruction, the selling of labourers into slavery, the sexual exploitation of African women and the plundering of villages for ivory and canoes. The accusation that he had taken an African woman as his mistress should be set beside the illustration to one of his books that shows him 'resisting temptation' in the form of an African woman.

18. 'African Exploration', *The Times*, 8 January 1876.

19. Neal Ascherson, *The King Incorporated: Leopold II in the Age of Trusts* (London: George Allen & Unwin, 1963), p. 47.

20. Quoted by Jocelyn Baines, *Joseph Conrad: A Critical Biography* (London: Weidenfeld & Nicolson, 1960; Harmondsworth: Penguin Books, 1971), p. 136.

21. Henry M. Stanley, *In Darkest Africa* (London, 1890), p. 50; hereafter cited as *DA*.

22. Shortly afterwards, however, Stanley came under attack from the Anti-Slavery Society at reports of his transporting unfree labourers from Zanzibar to the Congo. Subsequently, the Anti-Slavery Society criticized Stanley's association with Tippu Tib during the Lower Congo section of the expedition and the flogging of 'miscreants', the burning of villages and the enslavement or slaughter of their inhabitants that had accompanied his journey.

23. Norman Sherry, *Conrad's Western World* (Cambridge: Cambridge University Press, 1971), p. 14.

24. For more on Thys in relation to *Heart of Darkness*, see Gene M. Moore, 'Poradowska's *Yaga* and the Thys Libel Case', the *Conradian*, 18.1 (Autumn 1993), pp. 25–36.

25. For Conrad's own account of this journey, see *The Congo Diary* (pp. 147–61).

26. He recorded this journey in his 'Up-river Book', which is not included in this volume. Conrad was taken along as supernumerary to learn the route, and the 'Up-river Book' is very much a seaman's technical record for the navigation of the river. It is included in Zdzisław Najder (ed.), *Joseph Conrad: Congo Diary and Other Uncollected Pieces* (Garden City, N.Y.: Doubleday & Company, 1978), pp. 17–38, and in Robert Kimbrough (ed.), *Heart of Darkness* (New York: W.W. Norton & Company, 1988), pp. 167–86.

27. Notice that, in the manuscript, Kurtz is initially called 'Klein'.

28. He finished it on 6 February 1899, and it was serialized in *Blackwood's Magazine* from February to April. It was published in book form in 1902. For further details, see 'Note on the Text', pp. 3–7.

29. In the same way the manuscript version offers a much fuller description of Boma than is found in the printed text:

We went up some twenty miles and anchored off the seat of the government. I had heard enough in Europe about its advanced state of civilisation: the papers, nay the very paper vendors in the sepulchral city were boasting about the steam tramway and the hotel – especially the hotel. I beheld that wonder. It was like a symbol at the gate. It stood alone, a grey high cube of iron with two tiers of galleries outside towering above one of those ruinous-looking foreshores you come upon at home in out-of-the-way places where refuse is thrown out. To make the resemblance complete it wanted only a drooping post bearing a board with the legend: rubbish shot here, and the symbol would have had the clearness of the naked truth . . .

Conrad cuts away extraneous detail, elements of travelogue or memoir, to produce a more focused narrative and, by doing so, distances Marlow from his own personal experience.

30. In *Conrad's Western World*, for example, Norman Sherry made a good case for seeing some features of Kurtz's character and career as similar to those of Arthur Eugene Constant Hodister. Hodister had a charismatic reputation: he was a very successful ivory-trader, who did not bully but apparently charmed the ivory out of the Africans; he was one of the 'gang of virtue', who saw himself as having a mission beyond mere commercial enterprise; he was an explorer, whose eloquence revealed itself in his constant writing of reports; his enemies, however, suggested that he might have attended more African ceremonies than was altogether good for him. In his invaluable book *Conrad in the Nineteenth Century* (London: Chatto & Windus, 1980, hereafter cited as *CNC*), Ian Watt proposes other possible models for Kurtz, and then observes:

It is essential to the very nature of what Conrad was doing in *Heart of Darkness* that there should be not one but innumerable sources for Kurtz. Some of these have nothing to do with Africa or with Conrad's experiences there; but among those sources that do, Stanley is probably of central importance, though not so much as a basis for the character of Kurtz as for the moral atmosphere in which he was created. (p. 145)

Something of that moral atmosphere is suggested, on the one hand, by the scientific exploration of Franklin and McClintock and, on the other, by the distinctly 'militant geography' of Stanley.

31. See Cedric Watts, *Conrad's 'Heart of Darkness': A Critical and Contextual Discussion* (Milan: Mursia International, 1977), pp. 54–9, hereafter cited as Watts; Lillian Feder, 'Marlow's Descent into Hell',

Nineteenth-Century Fiction, 9.4 (March 1955), pp. 280–92; and Robert O. Evans, 'Conrad's Underworld', *Modern Fiction Studies*, 2.2 (May 1956), pp. 56–62. For Conrad's use of non-European cultural models, see W.B. Stein, 'The Heart of Darkness: A Bodhisattva Scenario', *Conradiana*, 2 (1969–70), pp. 39–52 and Peter Caracciolo, 'Buddhist Typologies in *Heart of Darkness* and *Victory*', the *Conradian*, 14.1/2 (December 1989), pp. 67–91.

32. See Watts, pp. 22–47, for a detailed discussion of the device.

33. Daphna Erdinast-Vulcan, *Joseph Conrad and the Modern Temper* (Oxford: Clarendon Press, 1991), p. 102.

34. *CNC*, p. 174.

35. ibid., pp. 175–80.

36. 'The device of delayed decoding simultaneously enacts the objective and the subjective aspects of moments of crisis', *CNC*, p. 179.

37. See Peter Brooks, *Reading for the Plot: Design and Intention in Narrative* (Cambridge, Mass.: Harvard University Press, 1984), pp. 238–63; hereafter cited as Brooks.

38. Conrad wrote to his agent, J.B. Pinker: 'There isn't a single club and messroom and man-of-war in the British Isles and Dominions which hasn't its copy of *Maga*' (November 1911). Even if this isn't an accurate account of *Blackwood's* readership, it nevertheless suggests the kind of readership Conrad assumed for *Heart of Darkness*.

39. Conrad to William Blackwood, 31 December 1898, in Frederick Karl and Laurence Davies (eds.), *The Collected Letters of Joseph Conrad* (Cambridge: Cambridge University Press, 1986), II, pp. 139–40.

40. Another telling detail is his embarrassed reference to the woman who has been forced to wash the shirts despite her 'distaste for the work'. This stands in contrast to the foreman of the mechanics ('a good worker'), who could be seen by the creek, rinsing 'with great care' the white serviette in which he wrapped his beard when he had to work in the mud under the bottom of the steamboat.

41. See Clive Hart, 'Wandering Rocks', in Clive Hart and David Hayman (eds.), *James Joyce's 'Ulysses'* (Berkeley and Los Angeles: University of California Press, 1974), pp. 181–216.

42. David Hannay, 'The Case of Mr Doughty', *Blackwood's Magazine* (June 1898), pp. 796–808. Hannay characterizes Drake as violent and self-seeking – and probably a murderer. Generally, he offers an unromantic and anti-heroic account of Elizabethan adventurers.

43. For a discussion of the way in which ideals turn into idols, and idolatry and fetishism become dominating tropes for the narrative, see Patrick Brantlinger, *Rule of Darkness: British Literature and Imperialism, 1830–1914* (Ithaca: Cornell University Press, 1988, hereafter cited as Brantlinger).

44. See Jeremy Hawthorn, *Joseph Conrad: Language and Fictional Self-consciousness* (London: Edward Arnold, 1979).

45. Chinua Achebe, 'An Image of Africa: Racism in Conrad's *Heart of Darkness*', the *Massachussetts Review*, 18 (1977), pp. 782–94; reprinted in Achebe, *Hopes and Impediments* (London: Heinemann, 1988).

46. Fothergill, p. 49. Fothergill cites the instance of the black guard, who is assumed to be cautious because, 'white men being so much alike at a distance', he couldn't tell who Marlow was (*HD*, p. 33).

47. W. Holman Bentley, *Pioneering in the Congo*, 2 vols. (London: Religious Tract Society, 1900).

48. Edward Said, *Orientalism* (New York: Vintage Books, 1979), p. 6.

49. ibid., p. 8.

50. Benita Parry, *Conrad and Imperialism* (London: Macmillan, 1983), p. 1.

51. Talal Asad, 'The Concept of Cultural Translation in British Social Anthropology', in James Clifford and George E. Marcus (eds.), *Writing Culture: The Poetics and Politics of Ethnography* (Berkeley and Los Angeles: University of California Press, 1986), p. 159.

52. Quoted in Sherry, p. 121.

53. Eric Woods, 'A Darkness Visible: Gissing, Masterman, and the Metaphors of Class, 1880–1914' (unpublished Ph.D. thesis, University of Sussex, 1989).

54. Frances B. Singh, 'The Colonialistic Bias of *Heart of Darkness*', *Conradiana*, 10.1 (1978), pp. 41–54.

55. Brantlinger, p. 262.

56. Peter Hyland, 'The Little Woman in the *Heart of Darkness*', *Conradiana*, 20.1 (Spring 1988), pp. 3–11, hereafter cited as Hyland. More recently Jeremy Hawthorn has argued that, in *Heart of Darkness*, 'issues of gender are inextricably intertwined with matters of race and culture' (*Joseph Conrad: Narrative Technique and Ideological Commitment* [London: Edward Arnold, 1990], pp. 183–92, especially p. 183, hereafter cited as Hawthorn).

57. Johanna M. Smith, '"Too Beautiful Altogether": Patriarchal Ideology in *Heart of Darkness*', in Ross C. Murfin (ed.), '*Heart of Darkness': A Case Study in Contemporary Criticism* (New York: St Martin's Press, 1989), pp. 179–98.

58. Nina Pelikan Straus, 'The Exclusion of the Intended from Secret Sharing in Conrad's *Heart of Darkness*', *Novel*, 20.2 (Winter 1987), pp. 123–37, especially p. 124.

SELECT BIBLIOGRAPHY

Further Works by Joseph Conrad

'An Outpost of Progress' in *Tales of Unrest* (London: T. Fisher Unwin, 1898)

'Youth' in *Youth: A Narrative; and Two Other Stories* (London and Edinburgh: William Blackwood, 1902)

Lord Jim (London and Edinburgh: William Blackwood, 1900)

Chance (London: Methuen, 1913)

'Tales of the Sea' in *Notes on Life and Letters* (London: J. M. Dent, 1921)

'Geography and Some Explorers' in *Last Essays* (London: J. M. Dent, 1926)

Conrad's Letters

G. Jean-Aubry, *Joseph Conrad: Life and Letters* (London: Heinemann, 1927)

Conrad's Polish Background, ed. Zdzisław Najder (London: Oxford University Press, 1964)

Joseph Conrad's Letters to Cunninghame Graham, ed. C. T. Watts (Cambridge: Cambridge University Press, 1969)

The Collected Letters of Joseph Conrad, ed. Frederick Karl and Laurence Davies (Cambridge: Cambridge University Press, 1983 onwards)

Biographies

Jocelyn Baines, *Joseph Conrad: A Critical Biography* (London: Weidenfeld & Nicolson, 1960; Harmondsworth: Penguin Books, 1971)

Owen Knowles, *A Conrad Chronology* (Basingstoke: Macmillan, 1989)

Zdzisław Najder, *Joseph Conrad: A Chronicle* (Cambridge: Cambridge University Press, 1983)

Zadzisław Najder (ed.), *Conrad Under Familial Eyes* (Cambridge: Cambridge University Press, 1983)

Martin Ray (ed.), *Joseph Conrad: Interviews and Recollections* (Basingstoke: Macmillan, 1990)

Cedric Watts, *Joseph Conrad: A Literary Life* (Basingstoke: Macmillan, 1989)

Criticism

GENERAL

Jacques Berthoud, *Joseph Conrad: The Major Phase* (Cambridge: Cambridge University Press, 1978)

William W. Bonney, *Thorns & Arabesques* (Baltimore: Johns Hopkins University Press, 1980)

Keith Carabine (ed.), *Joseph Conrad: Critical Assessments* (Robertsbridge: Helm Information, 1992)

Aaron Fogel, *Coercion to Speak: Conrad's Poetics of Dialogue* (Cambridge, Mass.: Harvard University Press, 1985)

R.A. Gekoski, *Conrad: The Moral World of the Novelist* (London: Elek, 1978)

Albert Guerard, *Conrad the Novelist* (Cambridge, Mass.: Harvard University Press, 1958)

James Guetti, *The Limits of Metaphor: A Study of Melville, Conrad, and Faulkner* (Ithaca, N.Y.: Cornell University Press, 1967)

Robert Hampson, *Joseph Conrad: Betrayal and Identity* (Basingstoke: Macmillan, 1992)

Jeremy Hawthorn, *Joseph Conrad: Language and Fictional Self-consciousness* (London: Edward Arnold, 1979)
Joseph Conrad: Narrative Technique and Ideological Commitment (London: Edward Arnold, 1990)

Bruce Johnson, *Conrad's Models of Mind* (Minneapolis: University of Minnesota Press, 1971)

J. Hillis Miller, 'Joseph Conrad' in *Poets of Reality: Six Twentieth-century Writers* (Cambridge, Mass.: Harvard University Press, 1966)

Ross C. Murfin (ed.), *Conrad Revisited* (University of Alabama Press, 1985)

Ruth L. Nadelhaft, *Joseph Conrad* (Hemel Hempstead: Harvester Wheatsheaf, 1991)

Benita Parry, *Conrad and Imperialism* (London: Macmillan, 1983)

Suresh Raval, *The Art of Failure: Conrad's Fiction* (London: Allen & Unwin, 1986)

Andrew Michael Roberts, *Conrad and Gender* (Amsterdam: Rodopi, 1993)

Norman Sherry, *Conrad's Western World* (Cambridge: Cambridge University Press, 1971)
(ed.) *Joseph Conrad: A Commemoration* (London: Macmillan, 1976)

Brian Spittles, *Joseph Conrad* (Basingstoke: Macmillan, 1992)

Ian Watt, *Conrad in the Nineteenth Century* (London: Chatto & Windus, 1980)

Cedric Watts, *A Preface to Conrad* (London: Longman, 1982)
The Deceptive Text: An Introduction to Covert Plots (Brighton: Harvester, 1984)

HEART OF DARKNESS CRITICISM

Chinua Achebe, 'An Image of Africa: Racism in Conrad's *Heart of Darkness*', *the Massachussetts Review*, 18.4 (Winter 1975); reprinted in Kimbrough, R. (ed.), *Heart of Darkness* (Norton edition, 1988)

Richard Adams, *Joseph Conrad: Heart of Darkness* (Harmondsworth: Penguin Books, 1991)

Harold Bloom (ed.), *Joseph Conrad's 'Heart of Darkness'* (New York: Chelsea House, 1987)

Patrick Brantlinger, '*Heart of Darkness*: Anti-Imperialism, Racism, or Impressionism?', *Criticism*, 27.4 (1985), pp. 363–85

Peter Brooks, 'An Unreadable Report: Conrad's *Heart of Darkness*' in *Reading for the Plot* (Cambridge, Mass.: Harvard University Press, 1984)

Robert Burden, *Heart of Darkness* (Basingstoke: Macmillan, 1991)

C.B. Cox (ed.), *Conrad: 'Heart of Darkness', 'Nostromo', and 'Under Western Eyes': A Casebook* (London: Macmillan, 1981)

Robert O. Evans, 'Conrad's Underworld', *Modern Fiction Studies*, 2.2 (1956), pp. 56–62

Lillian Feder, 'Marlow's Descent into Hell', *Nineteenth-Century Fiction*, 9.4 (1955), pp. 280–92

Anthony Fothergill, *Heart of Darkness* (Milton Keynes: Open University Press, 1989)

Robert Hampson, 'Conrad and the Idea of Empire', *L'Époque Conradienne* (Limoges: Société Conradienne Française, 1989), pp. 9–22

'*Heart of Darkness* and 'The Speech that Cannot be Silenced', *English*, 39.163 (Spring 1990), pp. 15–32

Hunt Hawkins, 'Conrad's Critique of Imperialism in *Heart of Darkness*', *PMLA*, 94.2 (1979), pp. 286–99

Peter Hyland, 'The Little Woman in the *Heart of Darkness*', *Conradiana*, 20.1 (1988), pp. 3–11

Ross C. Murfin (ed.), *'Heart of Darkness': A Case Study in Contemporary Criticism* (New York: St Martin's Press, 1989)

Jonah Raskin, 'Imperialism: Conrad's Heart of Darkness', *Journal of Contemporary History*, 2.2 (1967)

Frances B. Singh, 'The Colonialistic Bias of *Heart of Darkness*', *Conradiana*, 10.1 (1978); reprinted in Kimbrough, R. (ed.), *Heart of Darkness* (Norton edition, 1988)

Nina Pelikan Straus, 'The Exclusion of the Intended from Secret Sharing in Conrad's *Heart of Darkness*', *Novel*, 20.2 (1987), pp. 123–37

Jerome Thale, 'Marlow's Quest', *University of Toronto Quarterly*, 24.4 (1955), pp. 351–8

Jerry Wasserman, 'Narrative Presence: The Illusion of Language in *Heart of Darkness*', *Studies in the Novel*, 6.3 (1974), pp. 327–38

Cedric Watts, *Conrad's 'Heart of Darkness': A Critical and Contextual Discussion* (Milan: Mursia International, 1977)
    '"A Bloody Racist": About Achebe's View of Conrad', *Yearbook of English Studies*, 13 (1983), pp. 196–209

Colonialism and Literature

Francis Barker et al. (ed.), *Europe and Its Others* (Colchester, 1985)

Henry Louis Gates, *'Race', Writing and Difference* (Chicago: University of Chicago Press, 1986)

D.C.R.A. Goontilleke, *Developing Countries in British Fiction* (London: Macmillan, 1977)

Martin Green, *Dreams of Adventure, Deeds of Empire* (London: Routledge & Kegan Paul, 1980)

Abdul Jan Mohamed, *Manichean Aesthetics: The Politics of Literature in Colonial Africa* (Amherst, University of Massachusetts Press, 1983)

M.M. Mahood, *The Colonial Encounter* (London: Rex Collings, 1977)

J.A. McClure, *Kipling and Conrad: The Colonial Fiction* (Cambridge, Mass.: Harvard University Press, 1981)

Jeffrey Meyers, *Fiction and the Colonial Experience* (Ipswich: The Boydell Press, 1973)

Christopher L. Miller, *Blank Darkness: Africanist Discourse in French* (Chicago: University of Chicago Press, 1985)

Benita Parry, *Conrad and Imperialism* (London: Macmillan, 1983)

Jonah Raskin, *The Mythology of Imperialism* (New York: Random House, 1971)

Edward Said, *Orientalism* (New York: Random House, 1978)
The World, the Text, and the Critic (Cambridge: Cambridge University Press, 1983)
Culture and Imperialism (London: Chatto & Windus, 1993)

Alan Sandison, *The Wheel of Empire* (London: Macmillan, 1967)

Brian V. Street, *The Savage in Literature: Representations of 'Primitive' Society in English Fiction, 1858–1920* (London: Routledge & Kegan Paul, 1975)

Historical Material

NINETEENTH CENTURY

F. Leopold McClintock, *The Voyage of the 'Fox' in the Arctic Seas* (London: John Murray, 1859)

Dorothy, Lady Stanley (ed.), *The Autobiography of Sir Henry Morton Stanley* (1909)

H.M. Stanley, *How I Found Livingstone* (1872)
Through the Dark Continent, 2 vols. (1878)
In Darkest Africa, 2 vols. (1890)

TWENTIETH CENTURY

Neal Ascherson, *The King Incorporated: Leopold II in the Age of Trusts* (London: Allen & Unwin, 1963)

Felix Driver, 'Henry Morton Stanley and His Critics: Geography, Exploration and Empire', *Past & Present*, 133 (November 1991), pp. 134–66

V.G. Kiernan, *The Lords of Human Kind* (London: Century Hutchinson, 1969; 1988)

Thomas Pakenham, *The Scramble for Africa* (London: Weidenfeld & Nicolson, 1991; Abacus 1992)

HEART OF DARKNESS

NOTE ON THE TEXT

For this edition of *Heart of Darkness*, I have used as copy-text the text that appeared in *Youth: A Narrative; and Two Other Stories*, published by Blackwood's in 1902.

Conrad began writing the story in December 1898 and finished the first draft in February 1899. By this time the first instalment of 'The Heart of Darkness' had already appeared in the February 1899 issue of *Blackwood's Magazine*. Two further instalments appeared in March and April. This text was then revised for publication in book form, and it was included (under the title 'Heart of Darkness') with 'Youth' and 'The End of the Tether' in *Youth: A Narrative; and Two Other Stories* (Blackwood, 1902). All subsequent editions of *Heart of Darkness* derive from this edition.

The first American edition of *Youth: A Narrative; and Two Other Stories* was published by McClure, Phillips in 1903. The second British edition was published by J.M. Dent in 1917 with an 'Author's Note', which was also used for the later Dent collected 'editions' (the Uniform Edition, 1923; the Collected Edition, 1946) and is included in the present volume. In 1920 Doubleday brought out the first collected works of Conrad in a limited American edition (the 'Sun-Dial' Edition), and, in 1921, William Heinemann brought out *Youth: A Narrative; and Two Other Stories* as part of a limited British edition of the collected works. *Youth: A Narrative; and Two Other Stories* was subsequently published in 1923 by Doubleday in America and Dent in Britain as part of the first general collected 'editions'. Since both the Doubleday and the Dent editions were printed from plates originally made for the 'Sun-Dial' edition, they are thus issues of that edition.

There are three extant forms of the text prior to *Youth: A Narrative; and Two Other Stories* (1902): an incomplete manuscript, a section of typescript and the *Blackwood's Magazine* version. The manuscript, which is in the Houghton Library, Yale, begins just after the introduction of Marlow with the description of 'the yarns of seamen' (p. 18) and ends with Marlow's affirmation that Kurtz was 'a remarkable man' (p. 113). It is lightly punctuated and not divided into chapters. The most striking difference from the published text is the presence of passages like the description of the big steamer ('a long blaze of lights like a town') which passes the *Nellie* at the start of the narrative and the more extensive description of the 'seat of the government', which is presented in a much more particular and political way, with detailed attention to the tramway, the hotel and the daily customs of the government. Both these passages also appeared in the typescript but not in the serial text. The typescript, which is in the Henry W. and Albert A. Berg Collection, the New York Public Libraries, consists of thirty-four sheets and ends with the account of Marlowe's 'two-hundred-mile tramp' (p. 38) to the Central Station. Marion Michael and Wilkes Berry offer a detailed description of the typescript in 'The Typescript of *Heart of Darkness*', *Conradiana*, 12.2 (1980), pp. 147–55. They have identified it as the fragment of typescript sent by Conrad to David Meldrum, Blackwood's literary agent, on 9 January 1899, and, by a comparison with the manuscript, they demonstrate Jessie Conrad's collaboration in the production of the text through her reading and typing errors. Conrad subsequently revised the typescript to agree with the manuscript,

4

but either missed or adopted some of the changes: for example, the ensign of the French man-of-war, which had 'drooped limp' in the manuscript, 'dropped limp' in the typescript and subsequent texts.

For publication in book form in 1902 Conrad revised the serial text, but maintained the original division into instalments in the chapter divisions. The first instalment is only lightly revised: the most frequent change was the combining of single sentences into composite sentences through the replacement of full-stops by semicolons. The second instalment has even fewer changes. The final instalment, however, was quite extensively revised: in particular, the Harlequin's narrative, the description of the African woman, and the account of Marlow's encounter with Kurtz.

As a result of comparing the 1902 edition with earlier stages of the text, I have made a small number of changes. I have changed 'two-penny-halfpenny' to 'twopenny-halfpenny' (p. 28) and 'dumfounded' to 'dumbfounded' (p. 43): both readings were produced, in different ways, by line-breaks in the serial. Similarly, I have restored the comma between 'Gran' Bassam' and 'Little Popo', which was lost at a line end in the serial. I have also reinstated the manuscript reading 'a clear silk necktie' (p. 36) for 'a clear necktie'.

I have also incorporated the following, which were marked as corrections in Conrad's page-proofs for the Heinemann edition:

'has borne' for 'had borne' (p. 17)
'Trading Society' for 'Trading society' (p. 22)
'callipers' for 'calipers' (p. 27)
'perhaps – settlements' for 'perhaps. Settlements' (p. 29)
'trading-post' for 'trading post' (p. 37)
'Still, I passed' for 'Still I passed' (p. 39)

'You must' for 'you must' (p. 41)

'How can I tell' for 'How could I tell' (p. 43)

'I haven't even seen' for 'I hadn't even seen' (p. 43)

'Oh, those months!' for 'Oh, these months!' (p. 44)

'Anyway,' for 'Anyways,' (p. 45)

'in the moonlight;' for 'in the moonlight,' (p. 48)

'papier-mâché' for 'papier-maché' (p. 48)

'such impudence?' for 'such impudence.' (p. 56)

'then, pretending' for 'then pretending' (p. 59)

'the word "ivory"' for 'the word ivory' (p. 61)

'Fine sentiments' for 'Fine sentiments,' (p. 63)

'all be butchered' for 'be all butchered' (p. 69)

'to teach them,' for 'to teach them' (p. 69)

'a good tuck-in' for 'a good tuck in' (p. 70)

'Talking with . . .' for 'Talking with. . . .' (p. 79)

'trying to tell . . .' for 'trying to tell. . . .' (p. 80)

'new shoes?' for 'new shoes.' (p. 80)

'specimen was' for 'specimen, was' (p. 81)

'nerves went' for 'nerves, went' (p. 83)

'clean-up' for 'clean up' (p. 88)

'I sent' for 'I've sent' (p. 89)

'for the rest,' for 'for the rest' (p. 89)

'However,' for 'However' (p. 93)

'They would crawl . . .' for 'They would crawl. . . .' (p. 95)

'down-hill' for 'down hill' (p. 96)

'that means "short"' for 'that means short' (p. 97)

'in a shadowy embrace' for 'into a shadowy embrace' (p. 100)

'Nevertheless,' for 'Nevertheless' (p. 101)

'He suspected "there . . ."' for '"He suspected there . . ."'
   (p. 102)

'and then again . . .' for 'and then again. . . .' (p. 102)

'The fact is,' for 'The fact is' (p. 104)

'those ironic necessities' for 'these ironic necessities' (p. 117) 'grows quickly' for 'grows quick' (p. 119)

I have also followed later editions in changing the first edition's 'lounged' to 'lunged' (p. 77), even though this was Conrad's spelling in the manuscript.

R.G.H.

AUTHOR'S NOTE

The three stories in this volume[1] lay no claim to unity of artistic purpose. The only bond between them is that of the time in which they were written. They belong to the period immediately following the publication of the 'Nigger of the Narcissus,' and preceding the first conception of 'Nostromo,' two books which, it seems to me, stand apart and by themselves in the body of my work. It is also the period during which I contributed to *Maga*;[2] a period dominated by 'Lord Jim' and associated in my grateful memory with the late Mr William Blackwood's encouraging and helpful kindness.

'Youth' was not my first contribution[3] to *Maga*. It was the second. But that story marks the first appearance in the world of the man Marlow,[4] with whom my relations have grown very intimate in the course of years. The origins of that gentleman (nobody as far as I know had ever hinted that he was anything but that)—his origins have been the subject of some literary speculation of, I am glad to say, a friendly nature.

One would think that I am the proper person to throw a light on the matter; but in truth I find that it isn't so easy. It is pleasant to remember that nobody had charged him with fraudulent purposes or looked down on him as a charlatan; but apart from that he was supposed to be all sorts of things: a clever screen, a mere device, a 'personator,' a familiar spirit, a whispering 'dæmon.' I myself have been suspected of a meditated plan for his capture.

That is not so. I made no plans. The man Marlow and I came together in the casual manner of those health-resort acquaintances which sometimes ripen into friendships. This one has ripened. For all his assertiveness in matters of opinion he is not an intrusive person. He haunts my hours of solitude, when, in silence, we lay our heads together in great comfort and harmony; but as we part at the end of a tale I am never sure that it may not be for the last time. Yet I don't think that either of us would care much to survive the other. In his case, at any rate, his occupation would be gone[5] and he would suffer from that extinction, because I suspect him of some vanity. I don't mean vanity in the Solomonian sense.[6] Of all my people he's the one that has never been a vexation to my spirit. A most discreet, understanding man. . . .

Even before appearing in book-form 'Youth' was very well received. It lies on me to confess at last, and this is as good a place for it as another, that I have been all my life—all my two lives—the spoiled adopted child of Great Britain and even of the Empire; for it was Australia that gave me my first command.[7] I break out into this declaration not because of a lurking tendency to megalomania, but, on the contrary, as a man who has no very notable illusions about himself. I follow the instincts of vain-glory and humility natural to all mankind. For it can hardly be denied that it is not their own deserts that men are most proud of, but rather of their prodigious luck, of their marvellous fortune: of that in their lives for which thanks and sacrifices must be offered on the altars of the inscrutable gods.

'Heart of Darkness' also received a certain amount of notice from the first; and of its origins this much may be said: it is well known that curious men go prying into all sorts of places (where they have no business) and come out of them with all kinds of spoil. This story, and one other,[8] not in this volume, are all the spoil I brought out from the centre of Africa, where, really, I had no sort of business. More ambitious in its scope and longer in the telling, 'Heart of Darkness' is quite as authentic in fundamentals as 'Youth.' It is, obviously, written in another mood. I won't characterize the mood precisely, but anybody can see that it is anything but the mood of wistful regret, of reminiscent tenderness.

One more remark may be added. 'Youth' is a feat of memory. It is a record of experience; but that experience, in its facts, in its inwardness and in its outward colouring, begins and ends in myself. 'Heart of Darkness' is experience, too; but it is experience pushed a little (and only very little) beyond the actual facts of the case for the perfectly legitimate, I believe, purpose of bringing it home to the minds and bosoms of the readers. There it was no longer a matter of sincere colouring. It was like another art altogether. That sombre theme had to be given a sinister resonance, a tonality of its own, a continued vibration that, I hoped, would hang in the air and dwell on the ear after the last note had been struck.

After saying so much there remains the last tale of the book, still untouched. 'The End of the Tether' is a story of sea-life in a rather special way; and the most intimate thing I can say of it is this; that having lived that life fully, amongst its men, its thoughts and sensations, I have found it possible, without the slightest misgiving, in all sincerity of heart and peace of conscience, to conceive the existence of Captain Whalley's personality and to relate the manner of his end. This statement acquires some force from the circumstance that the pages of that story—a fair half of the book—are also the product of experience. That experience belongs (like 'Youth's') to the time before I ever thought of putting pen to paper. As to its 'reality,' that is for the readers to determine. One had to pick up one's facts here and there. More skill would have made them more real and the whole composition more interesting. But here we are approaching the veiled region of artistic values which it would be improper and indeed dangerous for me to enter. I have looked over the proofs, have corrected a misprint or two, have changed a word or two—and that's all. It is not very likely that I shall ever read 'The End of the Tether' again. No more need be said. It accords best with my feelings to part from Captain Whalley in affectionate silence.

J.C.
1917

Heart of Darkness

I

The *Nellie*,[1] a cruising yawl, swung to her anchor without a flutter of the sails, and was at rest. The flood had made, the wind was nearly calm, and being bound down the river, the only thing for it was to come to and wait for the turn of the tide.

The sea-reach of the Thames stretched before us like the beginning of an interminable waterway. In the offing the sea and the sky were welded together without a joint, and in the luminous space the tanned sails of the barges drifting up with the tide seemed to stand still in red clusters of canvas sharply peaked, with gleams of varnished sprits. A haze rested on the low shores that ran out to sea in vanishing flatness. The air was dark above Gravesend,[2] and farther back still seemed condensed into a mournful gloom, brooding motionless over the biggest, and the greatest, town on earth.[3]

The Director of Companies was our captain and our host. We four[4] affectionately watched his back as he stood in the bows looking to seaward. On the whole river there was nothing that looked half so nautical. He resembled a pilot,[5] which to a seaman is trustworthiness personified. It was difficult to realise his work was not out there in the luminous estuary, but behind him, within the brooding gloom.

Between us there was, as I have already said somewhere,[6] the bond of the sea. Besides holding our hearts together through long periods of separation, it had the effect of making us tolerant of each other's yarns – and even convictions. The Lawyer – the best of old fellows – had, because of his many years and many virtues, the only cushion on deck, and was lying on the only rug. The Accountant had brought out already a box of dominoes, and was toying architecturally with the bones.[7] Marlow sat cross-legged right aft, leaning against the mizzen-mast. He had sunken cheeks, a yellow complexion, a straight back, an ascetic aspect, and, with his arms dropped, the palms of hands outwards, resembled an idol.[8] The Director, satisfied the anchor had good hold, made his way aft and sat down amongst us. We exchanged a few words lazily. Afterwards there was silence on board the yacht. For some reason or other we did not begin that game of dominoes. We felt meditative, and fit for nothing but placid staring. The day was ending in a serenity of still and exquisite brilliance. The water shone pacifically; the sky, without a speck, was a benign immensity of unstained light; the very mist on the Essex marshes was like a gauzy and radiant fabric, hung from the wooded rises inland, and draping the low shores in diaphanous folds. Only the gloom to the west, brooding over the upper reaches, became more sombre every minute, as if angered by the approach of the sun.

And at last, in its curved and imperceptible fall, the sun sank low, and from glowing white changed to a dull red without rays and without heat, as if about to go out suddenly, stricken to death by the touch of that gloom brooding over a crowd of men.

Forthwith a change came over the waters, and the serenity became less brilliant but more profound. The old river in its broad reach rested unruffled at the decline of day, after ages of good service done to the race that peopled its banks, spread out in the tranquil dignity of a waterway leading to the uttermost ends of the earth. We looked at the venerable stream not in the vivid flush of a short day that comes and departs for ever, but in the august light of abiding memories. And indeed nothing is easier for a man who has, as the phrase goes, 'followed the sea' with reverence and affection, than to evoke the great spirit of the past upon the lower reaches of the Thames. The tidal current runs to and fro in its unceasing service, crowded with memories of men and ships it has borne to the rest of home or to the battles of the sea. It had known and served all the men of whom the nation is proud, from Sir Francis Drake[9] to Sir John Franklin,[10] knights all, titled and untitled – the great knights-errant of the sea. It had borne all the ships whose names are like jewels flashing in the night of time, from the *Golden Hind*[11] returning with her round flanks full of treasure, to be visited by the Queen's Highness and thus pass out of the gigantic tale, to the *Erebus* and *Terror*,[12] bound on other conquests – and that never returned. It had known the ships and the men. They had sailed from Deptford, from Greenwich, from Erith – the adventurers and the settlers; kings' ships and the ships of men on 'Change;[13] captains, admirals, the dark 'interlopers'[14] of the Eastern trade, and the commissioned 'generals'[15] of East India fleets. Hunters for gold or pursuers of fame, they all had gone out on that stream, bearing the sword, and often the torch, messengers of the might within the land, bearers of a spark from the sacred fire. What greatness had not floated on the ebb of that river into the mystery of an unknown earth! . . . The dreams of men, the seed of commonwealths, the germs of empires.

The sun set; the dusk fell on the stream, and lights began to appear along the shore. The Chapman lighthouse, a three-legged thing erect on a mudflat, shone strongly. Lights of ships moved in the fairway – a great stir of lights going up and going down. And farther west on the upper reaches the place of the monstrous town was still marked ominously on the sky, a brooding gloom in sunshine, a lurid glare under the stars.

'And this also,' said Marlow suddenly, 'has been one of the dark places of the earth.'[16]

He was the only man of us who still 'followed the sea.' The worst that could be said of him was that he did not represent his class. He was a seaman, but he was a wanderer too, while most seamen lead, if one may so express it, a sedentary life. Their minds are of the stay-at-home order, and their home is always with them – the ship; and so is their country – the sea. One ship is very much like another, and the sea is always the same. In the immutability of their surroundings the foreign shores, the foreign faces, the changing immensity of life, glide past, veiled not by a sense of mystery but by a slightly disdainful ignorance; for there is nothing mysterious to a seaman unless it be the sea itself, which is the mistress of his existence and as inscrutable as Destiny. For the rest, after his hours of work, a casual stroll or a casual spree on shore suffices to unfold for him the secret of a whole continent, and generally he finds the secret not worth knowing. The yarns of seamen have a direct simplicity, the whole meaning of which lies within the shell of a cracked nut. But Marlow was not typical (if his propensity to spin yarns be excepted), and to him the meaning of an episode was not inside like a kernel but outside, enveloping the tale which brought it out only as a glow brings out a haze, in the likeness of one of these misty halos that sometimes are made visible by the spectral illumination of moonshine.

His remark did not seem at all surprising. It was just like Marlow. It was accepted in silence. No one took the trouble to grunt even; and presently he said, very slow, –

'I was thinking of very old times, when the Romans first came here,[17] nineteen hundred years ago – the other day. . . .

Light came out of this river since – you say Knights?[18] Yes;
but it is like a running blaze on a plain, like a flash of lightning
in the clouds. We live in the flicker – may it last as long as the
old earth keeps rolling! But darkness was here yesterday.
Imagine the feelings of a commander of a fine – what d'ye call
'em? – trireme in the Mediterranean, ordered suddenly to the
north; run overland across the Gauls in a hurry; put in charge
of one of these craft the legionaries, – a wonderful lot of handy
men they must have been too – used to build, apparently by
the hundred, in a month or two, if we may believe what we
read.[19] Imagine him here – the very end of the world, a sea
the colour of lead, a sky the colour of smoke, a kind of ship
about as rigid as a concertina – and going up this river with
stores, or orders, or what you like. Sandbanks, marshes, forests,
savages, – precious little to eat fit for a civilised man, nothing
but Thames water to drink. No Falernian wine[20] here, no
going ashore. Here and there a military camp lost in a wilderness, like a needle in a bundle of hay – cold, fog, tempests,
disease, exile, and death, – death skulking in the air, in the
water, in the bush. They must have been dying like flies here.
Oh yes – he did it. Did it very well, too, no doubt, and
without thinking much about it either, except afterwards to
brag of what he had gone through in his time, perhaps. They
were men enough to face the darkness. And perhaps he was
cheered by keeping his eye on a chance of promotion to the
fleet at Ravenna[21] by-and-by, if he had good friends in Rome
and survived the awful climate. Or think of a decent young
citizen in a toga – perhaps too much dice, you know – coming
out here in the train of some prefect, or tax-gatherer, or trader
even, to mend his fortunes. Land in a swamp, march through
the woods, and in some inland post feel the savagery, the utter
savagery, had closed round him, – all that mysterious life of
the wilderness that stirs in the forest, in the jungles, in the

hearts of wild men. There's no initiation either into such mysteries. He has to live in the midst of the incomprehensible, which is also detestable. And it has a fascination, too, that goes to work upon him. The fascination of the abomination – you know. Imagine the growing regrets, the longing to escape, the powerless disgust, the surrender, the hate.'

He paused.

'Mind,' he began again, lifting one arm from the elbow, the palm of the hand outwards, so that, with his legs folded before him, he had the pose of a Buddha preaching in European clothes and without a lotus-flower – 'Mind, none of us would feel exactly like this. What saves us is efficiency – the devotion to efficiency. But these chaps were not much account, really. They were no colonists; their administration was merely a squeeze, and nothing more, I suspect. They were conquerors, and for that you want only brute force – nothing to boast of, when you have it, since your strength is just an accident arising from the weakness of others. They grabbed what they could get for the sake of what was to be got.[22] It was just robbery with violence, aggravated murder on a great scale, and men going at it blind – as is very proper for those who tackle a darkness. The conquest of the earth, which mostly means the taking it away from those who have a different complexion or slightly flatter noses than ourselves, is not a pretty thing when you look into it too much. What redeems it is the idea only. An idea at the back of it; not a sentimental pretence but an idea; and an unselfish belief in the idea – something you can set up, and bow down before, and offer a sacrifice to. . . .'

He broke off. Flames glided in the river, small green flames, red flames, white flames,[23] pursuing, overtaking, joining, crossing each other – then separating slowly or hastily. The traffic of the great city went on in the deepening night upon the sleepless river.[24] We looked on, waiting patiently –

there was nothing else to do till the end of the flood; but it was only after a long silence, when he said, in a hesitating voice, 'I suppose you fellows remember I did once turn fresh-water sailor for a bit,' that we knew we were fated, before the ebb began to run, to hear about one of Marlow's inconclusive experiences.

'I don't want to bother you much with what happened to me personally,' he began, showing in this remark the weakness of many tellers of tales who seem so often unaware of what their audience would best like to hear; 'yet to understand the effect of it on me you ought to know how I got out there, what I saw, how I went up that river to the place where I first met the poor chap. It was the farthest point of navigation and the culminating point of my experience. It seemed somehow to throw a kind of light on everything about me – and into my thoughts. It was sombre enough too – and pitiful – not extraordinary in any way – not very clear either. No, not very clear. And yet it seemed to throw a kind of light.

'I had then, as you remember, just returned to London after a lot of Indian Ocean, Pacific, China Seas – a regular dose of the East – six years or so, and I was loafing about, hindering you fellows in your work and invading your homes, just as though I had got a heavenly mission to civilise you. It was very fine for a time, but after a bit I did get tired of resting. Then I began to look for a ship – I should think the hardest work on earth. But the ships wouldn't even look at me. And I got tired of that game too.

'Now when I was a little chap I had a passion for maps.[25] I would look for hours at South America, or Africa, or Australia, and lose myself in all the glories of exploration. At that time there were many blank spaces[26] on the earth, and when I saw one that looked particularly inviting on a map (but they all look that) I would put my finger on it and say, When I grow up I will go there. The North Pole was one of these places, I remember. Well, I haven't been there yet, and shall not try now. The glamour's off. Other places were scattered about the Equator, and in every sort of latitude all over the two hemispheres. I have been in some of them, and . . . well, we won't talk about that. But there was one yet – the biggest, the most blank, so to speak – that I had a hankering after.

'True, by this time it was not a blank space any more. It had got filled since my boyhood with rivers and lakes and names.[27] It had ceased to be a blank space of delightful mystery – a white patch for a boy to dream gloriously over. It had become a place of darkness. But there was in it one river especially, a mighty big river, that you could see on the map, resembling an immense snake uncoiled, with its head in the sea, its body at rest curving afar over a vast country, and its tail lost in the depths of the land. And as I looked at the map of it in a shop-window, it fascinated me as a snake would a bird – a silly little bird. Then I remembered there was a big concern, a Company for trade[28] on that river. Dash it all! I thought to myself, they can't trade without using some kind of craft on that lot of fresh water – steamboats! Why shouldn't I try to get charge of one. I went on along Fleet Street, but could not shake off the idea. The snake had charmed me.

'You understand it was a Continental concern, that Trading Society; but I have a lot of relations living on the Continent, because it's cheap and not so nasty as it looks, they say.

'I am sorry to own I began to worry them. This was already a fresh departure for me. I was not used to get things that way, you know. I always went my own road and on my own legs where I had a mind to go. I wouldn't have believed it of myself; but, then – you see – I felt somehow I must get there by hook or by crook. So I worried them. The men said "My dear fellow," and did nothing. Then – would you believe it? –

I tried the women. I, Charlie Marlow, set the women to work
– to get a job. Heavens! Well, you see, the notion drove me. I
had an aunt, a dear enthusiastic soul. She wrote: "It will be
delightful. I am ready to do anything, anything for you. It is a
glorious idea. I know the wife of a very high personage in the
Administration, and also a man who has lots of influence
with," &c., &c. She was determined to make no end of fuss to
get me appointed skipper of a river steamboat, if such was my
fancy.

'I got my appointment – of course; and I got it very quick.
It appears the Company had received news that one of their
captains had been killed in a scuffle with the natives. This was
my chance, and it made me the more anxious to go. It was
only months and months afterwards, when I made the attempt
to recover what was left of the body, that I heard the original
quarrel arose from a misunderstanding about some hens. Yes,
two black hens. Fresleven[29] – that was the fellow's name, a
Dane – thought himself wronged somehow in the bargain, so
he went ashore and started to hammer the chief of the village
with a stick. Oh, it didn't surprise me in the least to hear this,
and at the same time to be told that Fresleven was the
gentlest, quietest creature that ever walked on two legs. No
doubt he was; but he had been a couple of years already out
there engaged in the noble cause, you know, and he probably
felt the need at last of asserting his self-respect in some way.
Therefore he whacked the old nigger mercilessly, while a big
crowd of his people watched him, thunderstruck, till some
man, – I was told the chief's son, – in desperation at hearing
the old chap yell, made a tentative jab with a spear at the
white man – and of course it went quite easy between the
shoulder-blades. Then the whole population cleared into the
forest, expecting all kinds of calamities to happen, while, on
the other hand, the steamer Fresleven commanded left also in

a bad panic, in charge of the engineer, I believe. Afterwards
nobody seemed to trouble much about Fresleven's remains, till
I got out and stepped into his shoes.[30] I couldn't let it rest,
though; but when an opportunity offered at last to meet my
predecessor, the grass growing through his ribs was tall enough
to hide his bones. They were all there. The supernatural
being[31] had not been touched after he fell. And the village was
deserted, the huts gaped black, rotting, all askew within the
fallen enclosures. A calamity had come to it, sure enough. The
people had vanished. Mad terror had scattered them, men,
women, and children, through the bush, and they had never
returned. What became of the hens I don't know either. I
should think the cause of progress got them, anyhow. However,
through this glorious affair I got my appointment, before I
had fairly begun to hope for it.

'I flew around like mad to get ready, and before forty-eight
hours I was crossing the Channel to show myself to my
employers, and sign the contract. In a very few hours I arrived
in a city that always makes me think of a whited sepulchre.[32]
Prejudice no doubt. I had no difficulty in finding the Company's offices.[33] It was the biggest thing in the town, and
everybody I met was full of it. They were going to run an
over-sea empire, and make no end of coin by trade.

'A narrow and deserted street in deep shadow, high houses,
innumerable windows with venetian blinds, a dead silence,
grass sprouting between the stones, imposing carriage archways
right and left, immense double doors standing ponderously
ajar. I slipped through one of these cracks, went up a swept
and ungarnished staircase, as arid as a desert, and opened the
first door I came to. Two women, one fat and the other slim,
sat on straw-bottomed chairs, knitting black wool.[34] The slim
one got up and walked straight at me – still knitting with
downcast eyes – and only just as I began to think of getting

out of her way, as you would for a somnambulist, stood still, and looked up. Her dress was as plain as an umbrella-cover, and she turned round without a word and preceded me into a waiting-room. I gave my name, and looked about. Deal table in the middle, plain chairs all round the walls, on one end a large shining map, marked with all the colours of a rainbow. There was a vast amount of red[35] – good to see at any time, because one knows that some real work is done in there, a deuce of a lot of blue, a little green, smears of orange, and, on the East Coast, a purple patch, to show where the jolly pioneers of progress drink the jolly lager-beer.[36] However, I wasn't going into any of these. I was going into the yellow. Dead in the centre. And the river was there – fascinating – deadly – like a snake. Ough! A door opened, a white-haired secretarial head, but wearing a compassionate expression, appeared, and a skinny forefinger beckoned me into the sanctuary. Its light was dim, and a heavy writing-desk squatted in the middle. From behind that structure came out an impression of pale plumpness in a frock-coat. The great man himself. He was five feet six, I should judge, and had his grip on the handle-end of ever so many millions. He shook hands, I fancy, murmured vaguely, was satisfied with my French. *Bon voyage.*

'In about forty-five seconds I found myself again in the waiting-room with the compassionate secretary, who, full of desolation and sympathy, made me sign some document. I believe I undertook amongst other things not to disclose any trade secrets. Well, I am not going to.

'I began to feel slightly uneasy. You know I am not used to such ceremonies, and there was something ominous in the atmosphere. It was just as though I had been let into some conspiracy – I don't know – something not quite right; and I was glad to get out. In the outer room the two women knitted black wool feverishly. People were arriving, and the younger one was walking back and forth introducing them. The old one sat on her chair. Her flat cloth slippers were propped up on a foot-warmer, and a cat reposed on her lap. She wore a starched white affair on her head, had a wart on one cheek, and silver-rimmed spectacles hung on the tip of her nose. She glanced at me above the glasses. The swift and indifferent placidity of that look troubled me. Two youths with foolish and cheery countenances were being piloted over, and she threw at them the same quick glance of unconcerned wisdom.[37] She seemed to know all about them and about me too. An eerie feeling came over me. She seemed uncanny and fateful. Often far away there I thought of these two, guarding the door of Darkness,[38] knitting black wool as for a warm pall, one introducing, introducing continuously to the unknown, the other scrutinising the cheery and foolish faces with unconcerned old eyes. *Ave!* Old knitter of black wool. *Morituri te salutant.*[39] Not many of those she looked at ever saw her again – not half, by a long way.

'There was yet a visit to the doctor. "A simple formality," assured me the secretary, with an air of taking an immense part in all my sorrows. Accordingly a young chap wearing his hat over the left eyebrow, some clerk I suppose, – there must have been clerks in the business, though the house was as still as a house in a city of the dead, – came from somewhere upstairs, and led me forth. He was shabby and careless, with inkstains on the sleeves of his jacket, and his cravat was large and billowy, under a chin shaped like the toe of an old boot. It was a little too early for the doctor, so I proposed a drink, and thereupon he developed a vein of joviality. As we sat over our vermuths he glorified the Company's business, and by-and-by I expressed casually my surprise at him not going out there. He became very cool and collected all at once. "I am not such a fool as I look, quoth Plato to his disciples,"[40] he said

26

sententiously, emptied his glass with great resolution, and we rose.

'The old doctor felt my pulse, evidently thinking of something else the while. "Good, good for there," he mumbled, and then with a certain eagerness asked me whether I would let him measure my head. Rather surprised, I said Yes, when he produced a thing like callipers and got the dimensions back and front and every way, taking notes carefully. He was an unshaven little man in a threadbare coat like a gaberdine, with his feet in slippers, and I thought him a harmless fool. "I always ask leave, in the interests of science, to measure the crania[41] of those going out there," he said. "And when they come back too?" I asked. "Oh, I never see them," he remarked; "and, moreover, the changes take place inside, you know." He smiled, as if at some quiet joke. "So you are going out there. Famous. Interesting too." He gave me a searching glance, and made another note. "Ever any madness in your family?" he asked, in a matter-of-fact tone. I felt very annoyed. "Is that question in the interests of science too?" "It would be," he said, without taking notice of my irritation, "interesting for science to watch the mental changes of individuals, on the spot, but . . ." "Are you an alienist?"[42] I interrupted. "Every doctor should be – a little," answered that original, imperturbably. "I have a little theory which you Messieurs who go out there must help me to prove. This is my share in the advantages my country shall reap from the possession of such a magnificent dependency. The mere wealth I leave to others. Pardon my questions, but you are the first Englishman coming under my observation . . ." I hastened to assure him I was not in the least typical. "If I were," said I, "I wouldn't be talking like this with you." "What you say is rather profound, and probably erroneous," he said, with a laugh. "Avoid irritation more than exposure to the sun. Adieu. How do you English say, eh? Good-bye. Ah! Good-bye. Adieu. In the tropics one must before everything keep calm." . . . He lifted a warning forefinger. . . . "*Du calme, du calme. Adieu.*"

'One thing more remained to do – say good-bye to my excellent aunt. I found her triumphant. I had a cup of tea – the last decent cup of tea for many days – and in a room that most soothingly looked just as you would expect a lady's drawing-room to look, we had a long quiet chat by the fireside. In the course of these confidences it became quite plain to me I had been represented to the wife of the high dignitary, and goodness knows to how many more people besides, as an exceptional and gifted creature – a piece of good fortune for the Company – a man you don't get hold of every day. Good heavens! and I was going to take charge of a twopenny-half-penny river-steamboat with a penny whistle attached! It appeared, however, I was also one of the Workers, with a capital[43] – you know. Something like an emissary of light, something like a lower sort of apostle.[44] There had been a lot of such rot[45] let loose in print and talk just about that time, and the excellent woman, living right in the rush of all that humbug, got carried off her feet. She talked about "weaning those ignorant millions from their horrid ways," till, upon my word, she made me quite uncomfortable. I ventured to hint that the Company was run for profit.

'"You forget, dear Charlie, that the labourer is worthy of his hire,"[46] she said, brightly. It's queer how out of touch with truth women are. They live in a world of their own, and there had never been anything like it, and never can be. It is too beautiful altogether, and if they were to set it up it would go to pieces before the first sunset. Some confounded fact we men have been living contentedly with ever since the day of creation would start up and knock the whole thing over.

'After this I got embraced, told to wear flannel, be sure to write often, and so on – and I left. In the street – I don't know why – a queer feeling came to me that I was an impostor. Odd thing that I, who used to clear out for any part of the world at twenty-four hours' notice, with less thought than most men give to the crossing of a street, had a moment – I won't say of hesitation, but of startled pause, before this commonplace affair. The best way I can explain it to you is by saying that, for a second or two, I felt as though, instead of going to the centre of a continent, I were about to set off for the centre of the earth.[47]

'I left in a French steamer,[48] and she called in every blamed port they have out there, for, as far as I could see, the sole purpose of landing soldiers and custom-house officers. I watched the coast. Watching a coast as it slips by the ship is like thinking about an enigma. There it is before you – smiling, frowning, inviting, grand, mean, insipid, or savage, and always mute with an air of whispering, Come and find out. This one was almost featureless, as if still in the making, with an aspect of monotonous grimness. The edge of a colossal jungle, so dark-green as to be almost black, fringed with white surf, ran straight, like a ruled line, far, far away along a blue sea whose glitter was blurred by a creeping mist. The sun was fierce, the land seemed to glisten and drip with steam. Here and there greyish-whitish specks showed up, clustered inside the white surf, with a flag flying above them perhaps – settlements some centuries old, and still no bigger than pin-heads on the untouched expanse of their background. We pounded along, stopped, landed soldiers; went on, landed custom-house clerks to levy toll in what looked like a God-forsaken wilderness, with a tin shed and a flag-pole lost in it; landed more soldiers – to take care of the custom-house clerks, presumably. Some, I heard, got drowned in the surf; but whether they did or not, nobody seemed particularly to care. They were just flung out there, and on we went. Every day the coast looked the same, as though we had not moved; but we passed various places – trading places – with names like Gran' Bassam, Little Popo, names that seemed to belong to some sordid farce acted in front of a sinister backcloth. The idleness of a passenger, my isolation amongst all these men with whom I had no point of contact, the oily and languid sea, the uniform sombreness of the coast, seemed to keep me away from the truth of things, within the toil of a mournful and senseless delusion. The voice of the surf heard now and then was a positive pleasure, like the speech of a brother. It was something natural, that had its reason, that had a meaning. Now and then a boat from the shore gave one a momentary contact with reality. It was paddled by black fellows. You could see from afar the white of their eyeballs glistening. They shouted, sang; their bodies streamed with perspiration; they had faces like grotesque masks – these chaps; but they had bone, muscle, a wild vitality, an intense energy of movement, that was as natural and true as the surf along their coast. They wanted no excuse for being there. They were a great comfort to look at. For a time I would feel I belonged still to a world of straightforward facts; but the feeling would not last long. Something would turn up to scare it away. Once, I remember, we came upon a man-of-war anchored off the coast. There wasn't even a shed there, and she was shelling the bush. It appears the French had one of their wars[49] going on there-abouts. Her ensign dropped limp[50] like a rag; the muzzles of the long eight-inch guns[51] stuck out all over the low hull; the greasy, slimy swell swung her up lazily and let her down, swaying her thin masts. In the empty immensity of earth, sky, and water, there she was, incomprehensible, firing into a continent. Pop, would go one of the eight-inch guns; a small flame would dart and vanish, a little white smoke would disappear, a tiny projectile would give a feeble screech – and nothing happened. Nothing could happen. There was a touch of insanity in the proceeding, a sense of lugubrious drollery in the sight; and it was not dissipated by somebody on board assuring me earnestly there was a camp of natives – he called them enemies![52] – hidden out of sight somewhere.

'We gave her her letters (I heard the men in that lonely ship were dying of fever at the rate of three a–day) and went on. We called at some more places with farcical names, where the merry dance of death and trade goes on in a still and earthy atmosphere as of an overheated catacomb; all along the formless coast bordered by dangerous surf, as if Nature herself had tried to ward off intruders; in and out of rivers, streams of death in life, whose banks were rotting into mud, whose waters, thickened into slime, invaded the contorted mangroves, that seemed to writhe at us in the extremity of an impotent despair. Nowhere did we stop long enough to get a particular-ised impression, but the general sense of vague and oppressive wonder grew upon me. It was like a weary pilgrimage amongst hints for nightmares.

'It was upward of thirty days before I saw the mouth of the big river. We anchored off the seat of the government.[53] But my work would not begin till some two hundred miles farther on. So as soon as I could I made a start for a place thirty miles higher up.

'I had my passage on a little sea-going steamer. Her captain was a Swede,[54] and knowing me for a seaman, invited me on the bridge. He was a young man, lean, fair, and morose, with lanky hair and a shuffling gait. As we left the miserable little wharf, he tossed his head contemptuously at the shore. "Been living there?" he asked. I said, "Yes." "Fine lot these govern-ment chaps – are they not?" he went on, speaking English with great precision and considerable bitterness. "It is funny what some people will do for a few francs a-month. I wonder what becomes of that kind when it goes up country?" I said to him I expected to see that soon. "So-o-o!" he exclaimed. He shuffled athwart, keeping one eye ahead vigilantly. "Don't be too sure," he continued. "The other day I took up a man who hanged himself on the road. He was a Swede, too." "Hanged himself! Why, in God's name?" I cried. He kept on looking out watchfully. "Who knows? The sun too much for him, or the country perhaps."

'At last[55] we opened a reach. A rocky cliff appeared, mounds of turned-up earth by the shore, houses on a hill, others, with iron roofs, amongst a waste of excavations, or hanging to the declivity. A continuous noise of the rapids above hovered over this scene of inhabited devastation. A lot of people, mostly black and naked, moved about like ants. A jetty projected into the river. A blinding sunlight drowned all this at times in a sudden recrudescence of glare. "There's your Company's station,"[56] said the Swede, pointing to three wooden barrack-like structures on the rocky slope. "I will send your things up. Four boxes did you say? So. Farewell."

'I came upon a boiler wallowing in the grass, then found a path leading up the hill. It turned aside for the boulders, and also for an undersized railway-truck lying there on its back with its wheels in the air. One was off. The thing looked as dead as the carcass of some animal. I came upon more pieces of decaying machinery, a stack of rusty rails. To the left a clump of trees made a shady spot, where dark things seemed to stir feebly. I blinked, the path was steep. A horn tooted to the right, and I saw the black people run. A heavy and dull detonation shook the ground, a puff of smoke came out of the cliff, and that was all. No change appeared on the face of the rock. They were building a railway.[57] The cliff was not in the way or anything; but this objectless blasting was all the work going on.

'A slight clinking behind me made me turn my head. Six black men advanced in a file, toiling up the path. They walked erect and slow, balancing small baskets full of earth on their heads, and the clink kept time with their footsteps. Black rags were wound round their loins, and the short ends behind wagged to and fro like tails. I could see every rib, the joints of their limbs were like knots in a rope; each had an iron collar on his neck, and all were connected together with a chain whose bights swung between them, rhythmically clinking. Another report from the cliff made me think suddenly of that ship of war I had seen firing into a continent. It was the same kind of ominous voice; but these men could by no stretch of imagination be called enemies. They were called criminals, and the outraged law, like the bursting shells, had come to them, an insoluble mystery from over the sea. All their meagre breasts panted together, the violently dilated nostrils quivered, the eyes stared stonily up-hill. They passed me within six inches, without a glance, with that complete, deathlike indifference of unhappy savages. Behind this raw matter one of the reclaimed, the product of the new forces at work, strolled despondently, carrying a rifle by its middle. He had a uniform jacket with one button off, and seeing a white man on the path, hoisted his weapon to his shoulder with alacrity. This was simple prudence, white men being so much alike at a distance that he could not tell who I might be. He was speedily reassured, and with a large, white, rascally grin, and a glance at his charge, seemed to take me into partnership in his exalted trust. After all, I also was a part of the great cause of these high and just proceedings.

'Instead of going up, I turned and descended to the left. My idea was to let that chain-gang get out of sight before I climbed the hill. You know I am not particularly tender; I've had to strike and to fend off. I've had to resist and to attack sometimes – that's only one way of resisting – without counting the exact cost, according to the demands of such sort of life as I had blundered into. I've seen the devil of violence, and the devil of greed, and the devil of hot desire; but, by all the stars! these were strong, lusty, red-eyed devils, that swayed and drove men – men, I tell you. But as I stood on this hillside, I foresaw that in the blinding sunshine of that land I would become acquainted with a flabby, pretending, weak-eyed devil of a rapacious and pitiless folly. How insidious he could be, too, I was only to find out several months later and a thousand miles farther. For a moment I stood appalled, as though by a warning. Finally I descended the hill, obliquely, towards the trees I had seen.

'I avoided a vast artificial hole somebody had been digging on the slope, the purpose of which I found it impossible to divine. It wasn't a quarry or a sandpit, anyhow. It was just a hole. It might have been connected with the philanthropic desire of giving the criminals something to do. I don't know. Then I nearly fell into a very narrow ravine, almost no more than a scar in the hillside. I discovered that a lot of imported drainage-pipes for the settlement had been tumbled in there. There wasn't one that was not broken. It was a wanton smash-up. At last I got under the trees. My purpose was to stroll into the shade for a moment; but no sooner within than it seemed to me I had stepped into the gloomy circle of some Inferno.[58] The rapids were near, and an uninterrupted, uniform, head-long, rushing noise filled the mournful stillness of the grove, where not a breath stirred, not a leaf moved, with a mysterious sound – as though the tearing pace of the launched earth had suddenly become audible.

'Black shapes crouched, lay, sat between the trees, leaning

against the trunks, clinging to the earth, half coming out, half effaced within the dim light, in all the attitudes of pain, abandonment, and despair. Another mine on the cliff went off, followed by a slight shudder of the soil under my feet. The work was going on. The work! And this was the place where some of the helpers had withdrawn to die.[59]

'They were dying slowly – it was very clear. They were not enemies, they were not criminals, they were nothing earthly now, – nothing but black shadows of disease and starvation, lying confusedly in the greenish gloom. Brought from all the recesses of the coast in all the legality of time contracts, lost in uncongenial surroundings, fed on unfamiliar food, they sickened, became inefficient, and were then allowed to crawl away and rest. These moribund shapes were free as air – and nearly as thin. I began to distinguish the gleam of eyes under the trees. Then, glancing down, I saw a face near my hand. The black bones reclined at full length with one shoulder against the tree, and slowly the eyelids rose and the sunken eyes looked up at me, enormous and vacant, a kind of blind, white flicker in the depths of the orbs, which died out slowly. The man seemed young – almost a boy – but you know with them it's hard to tell. I found nothing else to do but to offer him one of my good Swede's ship's biscuits I had in my pocket. The fingers closed slowly on it and held – there was no other movement and no other glance. He had tied a bit of white worsted round his neck – Why? Where did he get it? Was it a badge – an ornament – a charm – a propitiatory act? Was there any idea at all connected with it? It looked startling round his black neck, this bit of white thread from beyond the seas.

'Near the same tree two more bundles of acute angles sat with their legs drawn up. One, with his chin propped on his knees, stared at nothing, in an intolerable and appalling manner: his brother phantom rested its forehead, as if over-come with a great weariness; and all about others were scattered in every pose of contorted collapse, as in some picture of a massacre or a pestilence. While I stood horror-struck, one of these creatures rose to his hands and knees, and went off on all-fours towards the river to drink. He lapped out of his hand, then sat up in the sunlight, crossing his shins in front of him, and after a time let his woolly head fall on his breastbone.

'I didn't want any more loitering in the shade, and I made haste towards the station. When near the buildings I met a white man, in such an unexpected elegance of get-up that in the first moment I took him for a sort of vision. I saw a high starched collar, white cuffs, a light alpaca jacket, snowy trousers, a clear silk necktie,[60] and varnished boots. No hat. Hair parted, brushed, oiled, under a green-lined parasol held in a big white hand. He was amazing, and had a penholder behind his ear.

'I shook hands with this miracle, and I learned he was the Company's chief accountant, and that all the book-keeping was done at this station. He had come out for a moment, he said, "to get a breath of fresh air." The expression sounded wonderfully odd, with its suggestion of sedentary desk-life. I wouldn't have mentioned the fellow to you at all, only it was from his lips that I first heard the name of the man who is so indissolubly connected with the memories of that time. More-over, I respected the fellow. Yes; I respected his collars, his vast cuffs, his brushed hair. His appearance was certainly that of a hairdresser's dummy; but in the great demoralisation of the land he kept up his appearance. That's backbone. His starched collars and got-up shirt-fronts were achievements of character. He had been out nearly three years; and, later on, I could not help asking him how he managed to sport such linen. He had just the faintest blush, and said modestly, "I've been teaching one of the native women about the station. It was difficult. She had a distaste for the work." Thus this man had verily accomplished something. And he was devoted to his books, which were in apple-pie order.[61]

'Everything else in the station was in a muddle, – heads, things, buildings. Strings of dusty niggers with splay feet arrived and departed; a stream of manufactured goods, rubbishy cottons, beads, and brass-wire set into the depths of darkness, and in return came a precious trickle of ivory.

'I had to wait in the station for ten days – an eternity. I lived in a hut in the yard, but to be out of the chaos I would sometimes get into the accountant's office. It was built of horizontal planks, and so badly put together that, as he bent over his high desk, he was barred from neck to heels with narrow strips of sunlight. There was no need to open the big shutter to see. It was hot there too; big flies buzzed fiendishly, and did not sting, but stabbed. I sat generally on the floor, while, of faultless appearance (and even slightly scented), perching on a high stool, he wrote, he wrote. Sometimes he stood up for exercise. When a truckle-bed with a sick man (some invalided agent from up-country) was put in there, he exhibited a gentle annoyance. "The groans of this sick person," he said, "distract my attention. And without that it is extremely difficult to guard against clerical errors in this climate."

'One day he remarked, without lifting his head, "In the interior you will no doubt meet Mr Kurtz."[62] On my asking who Mr Kurtz was, he said he was a first-class agent; and seeing my disappointment at this information, he added slowly, laying down his pen, "He is a very remarkable person." Further questions elicited from him that Mr Kurtz was at present in charge of a trading-post, a very important one, in the true ivory-country, at "the very bottom of there. Sends in as much ivory as all the others put together . . ." He began to write again. The sick man was too ill to groan. The flies buzzed in a great peace.

'Suddenly there was a growing murmur of voices and a great tramping of feet. A caravan had come in. A violent babble of uncouth sounds burst out on the other side of the planks. All the carriers were speaking together, and in the midst of the uproar the lamentable voice of the chief agent was heard "giving it up" tearfully for the twentieth time that day. . . . He rose slowly. "What a frightful row," he said. He crossed the room gently to look at the sick man, and returning, said to me, "He does not hear." "What! Dead?" I asked, startled. "No, not yet," he answered, with great composure. Then, alluding with a toss of the head to the tumult in the station-yard, "When one has got to make correct entries, one comes to hate those savages – hate them to the death." He remained thoughtful for a moment. "When you see Mr Kurtz," he went on, "tell him from me that everything here" – he glanced at the desk – "is very satisfactory. I don't like to write to him – with those messengers of ours you never know who may get hold of your letter – at that Central Station." He stared at me for a moment with his mild, bulging eyes. "Oh, he will go far, very far," he began again. "He will be a somebody in the Administration before long. They, above – the Council in Europe, you know – mean him to be."

'He turned to his work. The noise outside had ceased, and presently in going out I stopped at the door. In the steady buzz of flies the homeward-bound agent was lying flushed and insensible; the other, bent over his books, was making correct entries of perfectly correct transactions; and fifty feet below the doorstep I could see the still tree-tops of the grove of death.

'Next day I left that station at last, with a caravan of sixty men, for a two-hundred-mile tramp.

'No use telling you much about that. Paths, paths, every-where; a stamped-in network of paths spreading over the empty land, through long grass, through burnt grass, through thickets, down and up chilly ravines, up and down stony hills ablaze with heat; and a solitude, a solitude, nobody, not a hut. The population had cleared out[63] a long time ago. Well, if a lot of mysterious niggers armed with all kinds of fearful weapons suddenly took to travelling on the road between Deal and Gravesend, catching the yokels right and left to carry heavy loads for them, I fancy every farm and cottage there-abouts would get empty very soon. Only here the dwellings were gone too. Still, I passed through several abandoned villages. There's something pathetically childish in the ruins of grass walls. Day after day, with the stamp and shuffle of sixty pair of bare feet behind me, each pair under a 60-lb. load. Camp, cook, sleep, strike camp, march. Now and then a carrier dead in harness, at rest in the long grass near the path, with an empty water-gourd and his long staff lying by his side. A great silence around and above. Perhaps on some quiet night the tremor of far-off drums, sinking, swelling, a tremor vast, faint; a sound weird, appealing, suggestive, and wild – and perhaps with as profound a meaning as the sound of bells in a Christian country.[64] Once a white man in an unbuttoned uniform, camping on the path with an armed escort of lank Zanzibaris,[65] very hospitable and festive – not to say drunk. Was looking after the upkeep of the road, he declared. Can't say I saw any road or any upkeep, unless the body of a middle-aged negro, with a bullet-hole in the forehead, upon which I absolutely stumbled three miles farther on, may be considered as a permanent improvement. I had a white compan-ion[66] too, not a bad chap, but rather too fleshy and with the exasperating habit of fainting on the hot hillsides, miles away from the least bit of shade and water. Annoying, you know, to hold your own coat like a parasol over a man's head while he is coming-to. I couldn't help asking him once what he meant by coming there at all. "To make money, of course. What do you think?" he said, scornfully. Then he got fever, and had to be carried in a hammock slung under a pole. As he weighed sixteen stone I had no end of rows with the carriers. They jibbed, ran away, sneaked off with their loads in the night – quite a mutiny. So, one evening, I made a speech in English with gestures, not one of which was lost to the sixty pairs of eyes before me, and the next morning I started the hammock off in front all right. An hour afterwards I came upon the whole concern wrecked in a bush – man, hammock, groans, blankets, horrors. The heavy pole had skinned his poor nose. He was very anxious for me to kill somebody, but there wasn't the shadow of a carrier near. I remembered the old doctor, – "It would be interesting for science to watch the mental changes of individuals, on the spot." I felt I was becoming scientifically interesting. However, all that is to no purpose. On the fifteenth day I came in sight of the big river again, and hobbled into the Central Station.[67] It was on a back water surrounded by scrub and forest, with a pretty border of smelly mud on one side, and on the three others enclosed by a crazy fence of rushes. A neglected gap was all the gate it had, and the first glance at the place was enough to let you see the flabby devil was running that show. White men with long staves in their hands appeared languidly from amongst the buildings, strolling up to take a look at me, and then retired out of sight somewhere. One of them, a stout, excitable chap with black moustaches, informed me with great volubility and many digressions, as soon as I told him who I was, that my steamer was at the bottom of the river. I was thunderstruck. What, how, why? Oh, it was "all right." The "manager himself" was there. All quite correct. "Everybody had behaved splendidly! splendidly!" – "You must," he said in agitation, "go and see the general manager at once. He is waiting!"

'I did not see the real significance of that wreck at once. I fancy I see it now,[68] but I am not sure – not at all. Certainly the affair was too stupid – when I think of it – to be altogether natural. Still. . . . But at the moment it presented itself simply as a confounded nuisance. The steamer was sunk. They had started two days before in a sudden hurry up the river with the manager on board, in charge of some volunteer skipper, and before they had been out three hours they tore the bottom out of her on stones, and she sank near the south bank. I asked myself what I was to do there, now my boat was lost. As a matter of fact, I had plenty to do in fishing my command out of the river. I had to set about it the very next day. That, and the repairs when I brought the pieces to the station, took some months.

'My first interview with the manager was curious. He did not ask me to sit down after my twenty-mile walk that morning. He was commonplace in complexion, in feature, in manners, and in voice. He was of middle size and of ordinary build. His eyes, of the usual blue, were perhaps remarkably cold, and he certainly could make his glance fall on one as trenchant and heavy as an axe. But even at these times the rest of his person seemed to disclaim the intention. Otherwise there was only an indefinable, faint expression of his lips, something stealthy – a smile – not a smile – I remember it, but I can't explain. It was unconscious, this smile was, though just after he had said something it got intensified for an instant. It came at the end of his speeches like a seal applied on the words to make the meaning of the commonest phrase appear absolutely inscrutable. He was a common trader, from his youth up employed in these parts – nothing more. He was obeyed, yet he inspired neither love nor fear, nor even respect.

He inspired uneasiness. That was it! Uneasiness. Not a definite mistrust – just uneasiness – nothing more. You have no idea how effective such a . . . a . . . faculty can be. He had no genius for organising, for initiative, or for order even. That was evident in such things as the deplorable state of the station. He had no learning, and no intelligence. His position had come to him – why? Perhaps because he was never ill . . . He had served three terms of three years out there . . . Because triumphant health in the general rout of constitutions is a kind of power in itself. When he went home on leave he rioted on a large scale – pompously. Jack ashore – with a difference – in externals only. This one could gather from his casual talk. He originated nothing, he could keep the routine going – that's all. But he was great. He was great by this little thing that it was impossible to tell what could control such a man. He never gave that secret away. Perhaps there was nothing within him. Such a suspicion made one pause – for out there there were no external checks. Once when various tropical diseases had laid low almost every "agent" in the station, he was heard to say, "Men who come out here should have no entrails." He sealed the utterance with that smile of his, as though it had been a door opening into a darkness he had in his keeping. You fancied you had seen things – but the seal was on. When annoyed at meal-times by the constant quarrels of the white men about precedence, he ordered an immense round table[69] to be made, for which a special house had to be built. This was the station's mess-room. Where he sat was the first place – the rest were nowhere. One felt this to be his unalterable conviction. He was neither civil nor uncivil. He was quiet. He allowed his "boy" – an overfed young negro from the coast – to treat the white men, under his very eyes, with provoking insolence.

'He began to speak as soon as he saw me. I had been very

long on the road. He could not wait. Had to start without me. The up-river stations had to be relieved. There had been so many delays already that he did not know who was dead and who was alive, and how they got on – and so on, and so on. He paid no attention to my explanations, and, playing with a stick of sealing-wax, repeated several times that the situation was "very grave, very grave." There were rumours that a very important station was in jeopardy, and its chief, Mr Kurtz, was ill. Hoped it was not true. Mr Kurtz was . . . I felt weary and irritable. Hang Kurtz, I thought. I interrupted him by saying I had heard of Mr Kurtz on the coast. "Ah! So they talk of him down there," he murmured to himself. Then he began again, assuring me Mr Kurtz was the best agent he had, an exceptional man, of the greatest importance to the Company; therefore I could understand his anxiety. He was, he said, "very, very uneasy." Certainly he fidgeted on his chair a good deal, exclaimed, "Ah, Mr Kurtz!" broke the stick of sealing-wax and seemed dumbfounded by the accident. Next thing he wanted to know "how long it would take to" . . . I interrupted him again. Being hungry, you know, and kept on my feet too, I was getting savage. "How can I tell?" I said. "I haven't even seen the wreck yet – some months, no doubt." All this talk seemed to me so futile. "Some months," he said. "Well, let us say three months before we can make a start. Yes. That ought to do the affair." I flung out of his hut (he lived all alone in a clay hut with a sort of verandah) muttering to myself my opinion of him. He was a chattering idiot. Afterwards I took it back when it was borne in upon me startlingly with what extreme nicety he had estimated the time requisite for the "affair."

'I went to work the next day, turning, so to speak, my back on that station. In that way only it seemed to me I could keep my hold on the redeeming facts of life. Still, one must look about sometimes; and then I saw this station, these men strolling aimlessly about in the sunshine of the yard. I asked myself sometimes what it all meant. They wandered here and there with their absurd long staves in their hands, like a lot of faithless pilgrims[70] bewitched inside a rotten fence. The word "ivory" rang in the air, was whispered, was sighed. You would think they were praying to it. A taint of imbecile rapacity blew through it all, like a whiff from some corpse. By Jove! I've never seen anything so unreal in my life. And outside, the silent wilderness surrounding this cleared speck on the earth struck me as something great and invincible, like evil or truth, waiting patiently for the passing away of this fantastic invasion.

'Oh, those months! Well, never mind. Various things happened. One evening a grass shed full of calico, cotton prints, beads, and I don't know what else, burst into a blaze so suddenly that you would have thought the earth had opened to let an avenging fire consume all that trash. I was smoking my pipe quietly by my dismantled steamer, and saw them all cutting capers in the light, with their arms lifted high, when the stout man with moustaches came tearing down to the river, a tin pail in his hand, assured me that everybody was "behaving splendidly, splendidly," dipped about a quart of water and tore back again. I noticed there was a hole in the bottom of his pail.

'I strolled up. There was no hurry. You see the thing had gone off like a box of matches. It had been hopeless from the very first. The flame had leaped high, driven everybody back, lighted up everything – and collapsed. The shed was already a heap of embers glowing fiercely. A nigger was being beaten near by. They said he had caused the fire in some way; be that as it may, he was screeching most horribly. I saw him, later on, for several days, sitting in a bit of shade looking very sick and trying to recover himself: afterwards he arose and went out – and the wilderness without a sound took him into its bosom again. As I approached the glow from the dark I found myself at the back of two men, talking. I heard the name of Kurtz pronounced, then the words, "take advantage of this unfortunate accident." One of the men was the manager. I wished him a good evening. "Did you ever see anything like it – eh? it is incredible," he said, and walked off. The other man remained. He was a first-class agent, young, gentlemanly, a bit reserved, with a forked little beard and a hooked nose.[71] He was stand-offish with the other agents, and they on their side said he was the manager's spy upon them. As to me, I had hardly ever spoken to him before. We got into talk, and by-and-by we strolled away from the hissing ruins. Then he asked me to his room, which was in the main building of the station. He struck a match, and I perceived that this young aristocrat had not only a silver-mounted dressing-case but also a whole candle all to himself. Just at that time the manager was the only man supposed to have any right to candles. Native mats covered the clay walls; a collection of spears, assegais, shields, knives was hung up in trophies. The business intrusted to this fellow was the making of bricks – so I had been informed; but there wasn't a fragment of a brick anywhere in the station, and he had been there more than a year – waiting. It seems he could not make bricks without something, I don't know what – straw maybe.[72] Anyway, it could not be found there, and as it was not likely to be sent from Europe, it did not appear clear to me what he was waiting for. An act of special creation[73] perhaps. However, they were all waiting – all the sixteen or twenty pilgrims of them – for something; and upon my word it did not seem an uncongenial occupation, from the way they took it, though the only thing that ever came to them was disease – as far as I could see. They beguiled the time by backbiting and intriguing against each other in a foolish kind of way. There was an air of plotting about that station, but nothing came of it, of course. It was as unreal as everything else – as the philanthropic pretence of the whole concern, as their talk, as their government, as their show of work. The only real feeling was a desire to get appointed to a trading-post where ivory was to be had, so that they could earn percentages. They intrigued and slandered and hated each other only on that account, – but as to effectually lifting a little finger – oh, no. By heavens! there is something after all in the world allowing one man to steal a horse while another must not look at a halter. Steal a horse straight out. Very well. He has done it. Perhaps he can ride. But there is a way of looking at a halter[74] that would provoke the most charitable of saints into a kick.

'I had no idea why he wanted to be sociable, but as we chatted in there it suddenly occurred to me the fellow was trying to get at something – in fact, pumping me. He alluded constantly to Europe, to the people I was supposed to know there – putting leading questions as to my acquaintances in the sepulchral city, and so on. His little eyes glittered like mica discs – with curiosity, – though he tried to keep up a bit of superciliousness. At first I was astonished, but very soon I became awfully curious to see what he would find out from me. I couldn't possibly imagine what I had in me to make it worth his while.[75] It was very pretty to see how he baffled himself, for in truth my body was full of chills, and my head had nothing in it but that wretched steamboat business. It was evident he took me for a perfectly shameless prevaricator. At last he got angry, and, to conceal a movement of furious annoyance, he yawned. I rose. Then I noticed a small sketch in oils, on a panel, representing a woman, draped and blind-folded, carrying a lighted torch.[76] The background was sombre

– almost black. The movement of the woman was stately, and the effect of the torchlight on the face was sinister.

'It arrested me, and he stood by civilly, holding a half-pint champagne bottle (medical comforts) with the candle stuck in it. To my question he said Mr Kurtz had painted this – in this very station more than a year ago – while waiting for means to go to his trading-post. "Tell me, pray," said I, "who is this Mr Kurtz?"

'"The chief of the Inner Station," he answered in a short tone, looking away. "Much obliged," I said, laughing. "And you are the brickmaker of the Central Station. Every one knows that." He was silent for a while. "He is a prodigy," he said at last. "He is an emissary of pity, and science, and progress, and devil knows what else. We want," he began to declaim suddenly, "for the guidance of the cause intrusted to us by Europe, so to speak, higher intelligence, wide sympathies, a singleness of purpose." "Who says that?" I asked. "Lots of them," he replied. "Some even write that; and so *he* comes here, a special being, as you ought to know." "Why ought I to know?" I interrupted, really surprised. He paid no attention. "Yes. To-day he is chief of the best station, next year he will be assistant-manager, two years more and . . . but I daresay you know what he will be in two years' time. You are of the new gang – the gang of virtue. The same people who sent him specially also recommended you. Oh, don't say no. I've my own eyes to trust." Light dawned upon me. My dear aunt's influential acquaintances were producing an unexpected effect upon that young man. I nearly burst into a laugh. "Do you read the Company's confidential correspondence?" I asked. He hadn't a word to say. It was great fun. "When Mr Kurtz," I continued severely, "is General Manager, you won't have the opportunity."

'He blew the candle out suddenly, and we went outside.

The moon had risen. Black figures strolled about listlessly, pouring water on the glow, whence proceeded a sound of hissing; steam ascended in the moonlight; the beaten nigger groaned somewhere. "What a row the brute makes!" said the indefatigable man with the moustaches, appearing near us. "Serve him right. Transgression – punishment – bang! Pitiless, pitiless. That's the only way. This will prevent all conflagrations for the future. I was just telling the manager . . ." He noticed my companion, and became crestfallen all at once. "Not in bed yet," he said, with a kind of servile heartiness; "it's so natural. Ha! Danger – agitation." He vanished. I went on to the river-side, and the other followed me. I heard a scathing murmur at my ear, "Heap of muffs – go to." The pilgrims could be seen in knots gesticulating, discussing. Several had still their staves in their hands. I verily believe they took these sticks to bed with them. Beyond the fence the forest stood up spectrally in the moonlight, and through the dim stir, through the faint sounds of that lamentable courtyard, the silence of the land went home to one's very heart, – its mystery, its greatness, the amazing reality of its concealed life. The hurt nigger moaned feebly somewhere near by, and then fetched a deep sigh that made me mend my pace away from there. I felt a hand introducing itself under my arm. "My dear sir," said the fellow, "I don't want to be misunderstood, and especially by you, who will see Mr Kurtz long before I can have that pleasure. I wouldn't like him to get a false idea of my disposition. . . ."

'I let him run on, this papier-mâché Mephistopheles,[77] and it seemed to me that if I tried I could poke my forefinger through him, and would find nothing inside but a little loose dirt, maybe. He, don't you see, had been planning to be assistant-manager by-and-by under the present man, and I could see that the coming of that Kurtz had upset them both not a little. He talked precipitately, and I did not try to stop him. I had my shoulders against the wreck of my steamer, hauled up on the slope like a carcass of some big river animal. The smell of mud, of primeval mud, by Jove! was in my nostrils, the high stillness of primeval forest was before my eyes; there were shiny patches on the black creek. The moon had spread over everything a thin layer of silver – over the rank grass, over the mud, upon the wall of matted vegetation standing higher than the wall of a temple, over the great river I could see through a sombre gap glittering, glittering, as it flowed broadly by without a murmur. All this was great, expectant, mute, while the man jabbered about himself. I wondered whether the stillness on the face of the immensity looking at us two were meant as an appeal or as a menace. What were we who had strayed in here? Could we handle that dumb thing, or would it handle us? I felt how big, how confoundedly big, was that thing that couldn't talk, and perhaps was deaf as well. What was in there? I could see a little ivory coming out from there, and I had heard Mr Kurtz was in there. I had heard enough about it too – God knows! Yet somehow it didn't bring any image with it – no more than if I had been told an angel or a fiend was in there. I believed it in the same way one of you might believe there are inhabitants in the planet Mars. I knew once a Scotch sailmaker who was certain, dead sure, there were people in Mars. If you asked him for some idea how they looked and behaved, he would get shy and mutter something about "walking on all-fours." If you as much as smiled, he would – though a man of sixty – offer to fight you. I would not have gone so far as to fight for Kurtz, but I went for him near enough to a lie. You know I hate, detest, and can't bear a lie, not because I am straighter than the rest of us, but simply because it appals me. There is a taint of death, a flavour of mortality in lies, – which is exactly what I hate and detest in the world – what I want to forget. It makes me miserable and sick, like biting something rotten would do. Temperament, I suppose. Well, I went near enough to it by letting the young fool there believe anything he liked to imagine as to my influence in Europe. I became in an instant as much of a pretence as the rest of the bewitched pilgrims. This simply because I had a notion it somehow would be of help to that Kurtz whom at the time I did not see – you understand. He was just a word for me. I did not see the man in the name any more than you do. Do you see him? Do you see the story? Do you see anything? It seems to me I am trying to tell you a dream – making a vain attempt, because no relation of a dream can convey the dream-sensation, that commingling of absurdity, surprise, and bewilderment in a tremor of struggling revolt, that notion of being captured by the incredible which is of the very essence of dreams. . . .'

He was silent for a while.

'. . . No, it is impossible; it is impossible to convey the life-sensation of any given epoch of one's existence, – that which makes its truth, its meaning – its subtle and penetrating essence. It is impossible. We live, as we dream – alone. . . .'

He paused again as if reflecting, then added –

'Of course in this you fellows see more than I could then. You see me, whom you know. . . .'

It had become so pitch dark that we listeners could hardly see one another. For a long time already he, sitting apart, had been no more to us than a voice. There was not a word from anybody. The others might have been asleep, but I was awake. I listened, I listened on the watch for the sentence, for the word, that would give me the clue to the faint uneasiness inspired by this narrative that seemed to shape itself without human lips in the heavy night-air of the river.

'. . . Yes – I let him run on,' Marlow began again, 'and

think what he pleased about the powers that were behind me. I did! And there was nothing behind me! There was nothing but that wretched, old, mangled steamboat I was leaning against, while he talked fluently about "the necessity for every man to get on." "And when one comes out here, you conceive, it is not to gaze at the moon." Mr Kurtz was a "universal genius," but even a genius would find it easier to work with "adequate tools – intelligent men." He did not make bricks – why, there was a physical impossibility in the way – as I was well aware; and if he did secretarial work for the manager, it was because "no sensible man rejects wantonly the confidence of his superiors." Did I see it? I saw it. What more did I want? What I really wanted was rivets, by heaven! Rivets. To get on with the work – to stop the hole. Rivets I wanted. There were cases of them down at the coast – cases – piled up – burst – split! You kicked a loose rivet at every second step in that station yard on the hillside. Rivets had rolled into the grove of death. You could fill your pockets with rivets for the trouble of stooping down – and there wasn't one rivet to be found where it was wanted. We had plates that would do, but nothing to fasten them with. And every week the messenger, a lone negro, letter-bag on shoulder and staff in hand, left our station for the coast. And several times a week a coast caravan came in with trade goods, – ghastly glazed calico that made you shudder only to look at it, glass beads value about a penny a quart, confounded spotted cotton handkerchiefs. And no rivets. Three carriers could have brought all that was wanted to set that steamboat afloat.

'He was becoming confidential now, but I fancy my unresponsive attitude must have exasperated him at last, for he judged it necessary to inform me he feared neither God nor devil, let alone any mere man. I said I could see that very well, but what I wanted was a certain quantity of rivets – and rivets were what really Mr Kurtz wanted, if he had only known it. Now letters went to the coast every week. . . . "My dear sir," he cried, "I write from dictation." I demanded rivets. There was a way – for an intelligent man. He changed his manner; became very cold, and suddenly began to talk about a hippo-potamus; wondered whether sleeping on board the steamer (I stuck to my salvage night and day) I wasn't disturbed. There was an old hippo that had the bad habit of getting out on the bank and roaming at night over the station grounds. The pilgrims used to turn out in a body and empty every rifle they could lay hands on at him. Some even had sat up o' nights for him. All this energy was wasted, though. "That animal has a charmed life," he said; "but you can say this only of brutes in this country. No man – you apprehend me? – no man here bears a charmed life." He stood there for a moment in the moonlight with his delicate hooked nose set a little askew, and his mica eyes glittering without a wink, then, with a curt Good night, he strode off. I could see he was disturbed and consider-ably puzzled, which made me feel more hopeful than I had been for days. It was a great comfort to turn from that chap to my influential friend, the battered, twisted, ruined, tin-pot steamboat. I clambered on board. She rang under my feet like an empty Huntley & Palmer biscuit-tin kicked along a gutter; she was nothing so solid in make, and rather less pretty in shape, but I had expended enough hard work on her to make me love her. No influential friend would have served me better. She had given me a chance to come out a bit – to find out what I could do. No, I don't like work. I had rather laze about and think of all the fine things that can be done. I don't like work – no man does – but I like what is in the work, – the chance to find yourself. Your own reality – for yourself, not for others – what no other man can ever know. They can only see the mere show, and never can tell what it really means.

'I was not surprised to see somebody sitting aft, on the deck, with his legs dangling over the mud. You see I rather chummed with the few mechanics there were in that station, whom the other pilgrims naturally despised – on account of their imperfect manners, I suppose. This was the foreman – a boiler-maker by trade – a good worker. He was a lank, bony, yellow-faced man, with big intense eyes. His aspect was worried, and his head was as bald as the palm of my hand; but his hair in falling seemed to have stuck to his chin, and had prospered in the new locality, for his beard hung down to his waist. He was a widower with six young children (he had left them in charge of a sister of his to come out there), and the passion of his life was pigeon-flying. He was an enthusiast and a connoisseur. He would rave about pigeons. After work hours he used sometimes to come over from his hut for a talk about his children and his pigeons; at work, when he had to crawl in the mud under the bottom of the steamboat, he would tie up that beard of his in a kind of white serviette he brought for the purpose. It had loops to go over his ears. In the evening he could be seen squatted on the bank rinsing that wrapper in the creek with great care, then spreading it solemnly on a bush to dry.

'I slapped him on the back and shouted "We shall have rivets!" He scrambled to his feet exclaiming "No! Rivets!" as though he couldn't believe his ears. Then in a low voice, "You . . . eh?" I don't know why we behaved like lunatics. I put my finger to the side of my nose and nodded mysteriously. "Good for you!" he cried, snapped his fingers above his head, lifting one foot. I tried a jig. We capered on the iron deck. A frightful clatter came out of that hulk, and the virgin forest on the other bank of the creek sent it back in a thundering roll upon the sleeping station. It must have made some of the pilgrims sit up in their hovels. A dark figure obscured the lighted doorway of

53

the manager's hut, vanished, then, a second or so after, the doorway itself vanished too. We stopped, and the silence driven away by the stamping of our feet flowed back again from the recesses of the land. The great wall of vegetation, an exuberant and entangled mass of trunks, branches, leaves, boughs, festoons, motionless in the moonlight, was like a rioting invasion of soundless life, a rolling wave of plants, piled up, crested, ready to topple over the creek, to sweep every little man of us out of his little existence. And it moved not. A deadened burst of mighty splashes and snorts reached us from afar, as though an ichthyosaurus[78] had been taking a bath of glitter in the great river. "After all," said the boiler-maker in a reasonable tone, "why shouldn't we get the rivets?" Why not, indeed! I did not know of any reason why we shouldn't. "They'll come in three weeks," I said, confidently.

'But they didn't. Instead of rivets there came an invasion, an infliction, a visitation. It came in sections during the next three weeks, each section headed by a donkey carrying a white man in new clothes and tan shoes, bowing from that elevation right and left to the impressed pilgrims. A quarrelsome band of footsore sulky niggers trod on the heels of the donkey; a lot of tents, camp-stools, tin boxes, white cases, brown bales would be shot down in the courtyard, and the air of mystery would deepen a little over the muddle of the station. Five such instalments came, with their absurd air of disorderly flight with the loot of innumerable outfit shops and provision stores, that, one would think, they were lugging, after a raid, into the wilderness for equitable division. It was an inextricable mess of things decent in themselves but that human folly made look like the spoils of thieving.

'This devoted band called itself the Eldorado[79] Exploring Expedition,[80] and I believe they were sworn to secrecy. Their talk, however, was the talk of sordid buccaneers: it was reckless

54

without hardihood, greedy without audacity, and cruel without courage; there was not an atom of foresight or of serious intention in the whole batch of them, and they did not seem aware these things are wanted for the work of the world. To tear treasure out of the bowels of the land was their desire, with no more moral purpose at the back of it than there is in burglars breaking into a safe. Who paid the expenses of the noble enterprise I don't know; but the uncle of our manager was leader of that lot.

'In exterior he resembled a butcher in a poor neighbour-hood, and his eyes had a look of sleepy cunning. He carried his fat paunch with ostentation on his short legs, and during the time his gang infested the station spoke to no one but his nephew. You could see these two roaming about all day long with their heads close together in an everlasting confab.

'I had given up worrying myself about the rivets. One's capacity for that kind of folly is more limited than you would suppose. I said Hang! – and let things slide. I had plenty of time for meditation, and now and then I would give some thought to Kurtz. I wasn't very interested in him. No. Still, I was curious to see whether this man, who had come out equipped with moral ideas of some sort, would climb to the top after all, and how he would set about his work when there.'

2

'One evening as I was lying flat on the deck of my steamboat, I heard voices approaching – and there were the nephew and the uncle strolling along the bank. I laid my head on my arm again, and had nearly lost myself in a doze, when somebody said in my ear, as it were: "I am as harmless as a little child, but I don't like to be dictated to. Am I the manager – or am I not? I was ordered to send him there. It's incredible." ... I became aware that the two were standing on the shore along-side the forepart of the steamboat, just below my head. I did not move; it did not occur to me to move: I was sleepy. "It *is* unpleasant," grunted the uncle. "He has asked the Administration to be sent there," said the other, "with the idea of showing what he could do; and I was instructed accordingly. Look at the influence that man must have. Is it not frightful?" They both agreed it was frightful, then made several bizarre remarks: "Make rain and fine weather[81] – one man – the Council – by the nose" – bits of absurd sentences that got the better of my drowsiness, so that I had pretty near the whole of my wits about me when the uncle said, "The climate may do away with this difficulty for you. Is he alone there?" "Yes," answered the manager; "he sent his assistant down the river with a note to me in these terms: 'Clear this poor devil out of the country, and don't bother sending more of that sort. I had rather be alone than have the kind of men you can dispose of with me.' It was more than a year ago. Can you imagine such impudence?" "Anything since then?" asked the other, hoarsely. "Ivory," jerked the nephew; "lots of it – prime sort – lots – most annoying, from him." "And with that?" questioned the heavy rumble. "Invoice," was the reply fired out, so to speak. Then silence. They had been talking about Kurtz.

'I was broad awake by this time, but, lying perfectly at ease, remained still, having no inducement to change my position. "How did that ivory come all this way?" growled the elder man, who seemed very vexed. The other explained that it had come with a fleet of canoes in charge of an English half-caste clerk Kurtz had with him; that Kurtz had apparently intended to return himself, the station being by that time bare of goods and stores, but after coming three hundred miles, had suddenly decided to go back, which he started to do alone in a small dug-out with four paddlers, leaving the half-caste to continue down the river with the ivory. The two fellows there seemed astounded at anybody attempting such a thing. They were at a loss for an adequate motive. As to me, I seemed to see Kurtz for the first time. It was a distinct glimpse: the dug-out, four paddling savages, and the lone white man turning his back suddenly on the headquarters, on relief, on thoughts of home – perhaps; setting his face towards the depths of the wilderness, towards his empty and desolate station. I did not know the motive. Perhaps he was just simply a fine fellow who stuck to his work for its own sake. His name, you understand, had not been pronounced once. He was "that man." The half-caste, who, as far as I could see, had conducted a difficult trip with great prudence and pluck, was invariably alluded to as "that scoundrel." The "scoundrel" had reported that the "man" had been very ill – had recovered imperfectly. . . . The two below me moved away then a few paces, and strolled back and forth at some little distance. I heard: "Military post – doctor – two hundred miles – quite alone now – unavoidable delays – nine months – no news – strange rumours." They approached again, just as the manager was saying, "No one, as far as I know, unless a species of wandering trader – a pestilential fellow, snapping ivory from the natives." Who was it they were talking about now? I gathered in snatches that this was some man supposed to be in Kurtz's district, and of whom the manager did not approve. "We will not be free from unfair competition till one of these fellows is hanged for an example," he said. "Certainly," grunted the other; "get him hanged! Why not? Anything – anything can be done in this country. That's what I say; nobody here, you understand, *here*, can

endanger your position. And why? You stand the climate –
you outlast them all. The danger is in Europe; but there
before I left I took care to—" They moved off and whispered,
then their voices rose again. "The extraordinary series of
delays is not my fault. I did my possible." The fat man sighed,
"Very sad." "And the pestiferous absurdity of his talk,"
continued the other; "he bothered me enough when he was
here. 'Each station should be like a beacon on the road
towards better things, a centre for trade of course, but also for
humanising, improving, instructing.' Conceive you[82] – that
ass! And he wants to be manager! No, it's—" Here he got
choked by excessive indignation, and I lifted my head the least
bit. I was surprised to see how near they were – right under
me. I could have spat upon their hats. They were looking on
the ground, absorbed in thought. The manager was switching
his leg with a slender twig: his sagacious relative lifted his
head. "You have been well since you came out this time?" he
asked. The other gave a start. "Who? I? Oh! Like a charm –
like a charm. But the rest – oh, my goodness! All sick. They
die so quick, too, that I haven't the time to send them out of
the country – it's incredible!" "H'm. Just so," grunted the
uncle. "Ah! my boy, trust to this – I say, trust to this." I saw
him extend his short flipper of an arm for a gesture that took
in the forest, the creek, the mud, the river, – seemed to beckon
with a dishonouring flourish before the sunlit face of the land
a treacherous appeal to the lurking death, to the hidden evil, to
the profound darkness of its heart. It was so startling that I
leaped to my feet and looked back at the edge of the forest, as
though I had expected an answer of some sort to that black
display of confidence. You know the foolish notions that come
to one sometimes. The high stillness confronted these two
figures with its ominous patience, waiting for the passing away
of a fantastic invasion.

'They swore aloud together – out of sheer fright, I believe – then, pretending not to know anything of my existence, turned back to the station. The sun was low; and leaning forward side by side, they seemed to be tugging painfully uphill their two ridiculous shadows of unequal length, that trailed behind them slowly over the tall grass without bending a single blade.

'In a few days the Eldorado Expedition went into the patient wilderness, that closed upon it as the sea closes over a diver. Long afterwards the news came that all the donkeys were dead. I know nothing as to the fate of the less valuable animals. They, no doubt, like the rest of us, found what they deserved. I did not inquire. I was then rather excited at the prospect of meeting Kurtz very soon. When I say very soon I mean it comparatively. It was just two months from the day we left the creek when we came to the bank below Kurtz's station.

'Going up that river was like travelling back to the earliest beginnings of the world, when vegetation rioted on the earth and the big trees were kings. An empty stream, a great silence, an impenetrable forest. The air was warm, thick, heavy, sluggish. There was no joy in the brilliance of sunshine. The long stretches of the waterway ran on, deserted, into the gloom of overshadowed distances. On silvery sandbanks hippos and alligators sunned themselves side by side. The broadening waters flowed through a mob of wooded islands; you lost your way on that river as you would in a desert, and butted all day long against shoals, trying to find the channel, till you thought yourself bewitched and cut off for ever from everything you had known once – somewhere – far away – in another existence perhaps. There were moments when one's past came back to one, as it will sometimes when you have not a moment to spare to yourself; but it came in the shape of an unrestful and noisy dream, remembered with wonder amongst the overwhelming realities of this strange world of plants, and water, and silence. And this stillness of life did not in the least resemble a peace. It was the stillness of an implacable force brooding over an inscrutable intention. It looked at you with a vengeful aspect. I got used to it afterwards; I did not see it any more; I had no time. I had to keep guessing at the channel; I had to discern, mostly by inspiration, the signs of hidden banks; I watched for sunken stones; I was learning to clap my teeth smartly before my heart flew out, when I shaved by a fluke some infernal sly old snag that would have ripped the life out of the tin-pot steamboat and drowned all the pilgrims; I had to keep a look-out for the signs of dead wood we could cut up in the night for next day's steaming. When you have to attend to things of that sort, to the mere incidents of the surface, the reality – the reality, I tell you – fades. The inner truth is hidden – luckily, luckily. But I felt it all the same; I felt often its mysterious stillness watching me at my monkey tricks, just as it watches you fellows performing on your respective tight-ropes for – what is it? half-a-crown a tumble—'

'Try to be civil, Marlow,' growled a voice, and I knew there was at least one listener awake besides myself.

'I beg your pardon. I forgot the heartache which makes up the rest of the price. And indeed what does the price matter, if the trick be well done? You do your tricks very well. And I didn't do badly either, since I managed not to sink that steamboat on my first trip. It's a wonder to me yet. Imagine a blindfolded man set to drive a van over a bad road. I sweated and shivered over that business considerably, I can tell you. After all, for a seaman, to scrape the bottom of the thing that's supposed to float all the time under his care is the unpardonable sin. No one may know of it, but you never forget the thump – eh? A blow on the very heart. You remember it, you

dream of it, you wake up at night and think of it – years after
– and go hot and cold all over. I don't pretend to say that
steamboat floated all the time. More than once she had to
wade for a bit, with twenty cannibals[83] splashing around and
pushing. We had enlisted some of these chaps on the way for a
crew. Fine fellows – cannibals – in their place. They were men
one could work with, and I am grateful to them. And, after all,
they did not eat each other before my face: they had brought
along a provision of hippo-meat which went rotten, and made
the mystery of the wilderness stink in my nostrils. Phoo! I can
sniff it now. I had the manager on board and three or four
pilgrims[84] with their staves – all complete. Sometimes we
came upon a station close by the bank, clinging to the skirts of
the unknown, and the white men rushing out of a tumble-
down hovel, with great gestures of joy and surprise and
welcome, seemed very strange, – had the appearance of being
held there captive by a spell. The word "ivory" would ring in
the air for a while – and on we went again into the silence,
along empty reaches, round the still bends, between the high
walls of our winding way, reverberating in hollow claps the
ponderous beat of the stern-wheel. Trees, trees, millions of
trees, massive, immense, running up high; and at their foot,
hugging the bank against the stream, crept the little begrimed
steamboat, like a sluggish beetle crawling on the floor of a
lofty portico. It made you feel very small, very lost, and yet it
was not altogether depressing that feeling. After all, if you
were small, the grimy beetle crawled on – which was just what
you wanted it to do. Where the pilgrims imagined it crawled
to I don't know. To some place where they expected to get
something, I bet! For me it crawled towards Kurtz – exclusively;[85] but when the steam-pipes started leaking we crawled
very slow. The reaches opened before us and closed behind, as
if the forest had stepped leisurely across the water to bar the

way for our return. We penetrated deeper and deeper into the heart of darkness. It was very quiet there. At night sometimes the roll of drums behind the curtain of trees would run up the river and remain sustained faintly, as if hovering in the air high over our heads, till the first break of day. Whether it meant war, peace, or prayer[86] we could not tell. The dawns were heralded by the descent of a chill stillness; the wood-cutters slept, their fires burned low; the snapping of a twig would make you start. We were wanderers on a prehistoric earth, on an earth that wore the aspect of an unknown planet. We could have fancied ourselves the first of men taking possession of an accursed inheritance, to be subdued at the cost of profound anguish and of excessive toil. But suddenly, as we struggled round a bend, there would be a glimpse of rush walls, of peaked grass-roofs, a burst of yells, a whirl of black limbs, a mass of hands clapping, of feet stamping, of bodies swaying, of eyes rolling, under the droop of heavy and motionless foliage. The steamer toiled along slowly on the edge of a black and incomprehensible frenzy. The prehistoric man was cursing us, praying to us, welcoming us – who could tell? We were cut off from the comprehension of our surround-ings; we glided past like phantoms, wondering and secretly appalled, as sane men would be before an enthusiastic outbreak in a madhouse. We could not understand, because we were too far and could not remember, because we were travelling in the night of first ages, of those ages that are gone, leaving hardly a sign – and no memories.

'The earth seemed unearthly. We are accustomed to look upon the shackled form of a conquered monster, but there – there you could look at a thing monstrous and free. It was unearthly, and the men were— No, they were not inhuman. Well, you know, that was the worst of it – this suspicion of their not being inhuman. It would come slowly to one. They howled, and leaped, and spun, and made horrid faces; but what thrilled you was just the thought of their humanity – like yours – the thought of your remote kinship with this wild and passionate uproar. Ugly. Yes, it was ugly enough; but if you were man enough you would admit to yourself that there was in you just the faintest trace of a response to the terrible frankness of that noise, a dim suspicion of there being a meaning in it which you – you so remote from the night of first ages – could comprehend. And why not? The mind of man is capable of anything – because everything is in it, all the past as well as all the future. What was there after all? Joy, fear, sorrow, devotion, valour, rage – who can tell? – but truth – truth stripped of its cloak of time. Let the fool gape and shudder – the man knows, and can look on without a wink. But he must at least be as much of a man as these on the shore. He must meet that truth with his own true stuff – with his own inborn strength. Principles? Principles won't do. Acquisitions, clothes, pretty rags – rags that would fly off at the first good shake. No; you want a deliberate belief. An appeal to me in this fiendish row – is there? Very well; I hear; I admit, but I have a voice too, and for good or evil mine is the speech that cannot be silenced. Of course, a fool, what with sheer fright and fine sentiments, is always safe. Who's that grunting? You wonder I didn't go ashore for a howl and a dance? Well, no – I didn't. Fine sentiments, you say? Fine sentiments be hanged! I had no time. I had to mess about with white-lead and strips of woollen blanket[87] helping to put bandages on those leaky steam-pipes – I tell you. I had to watch the steering, and circumvent those snags, and get the tin-pot along by hook or by crook. There was surface-truth enough in these things to save a wiser man. And between whiles I had to look after the savage who was fireman. He was an improved specimen; he could fire up a vertical boiler.[88] He was there below me, and, upon my word, to look at him was as edifying as seeing a dog in a parody of breeches and a feather hat, walking on his hind-legs. A few months of training had done for that really fine chap. He squinted at the steam-gauge and at the water-gauge with an evident effort of intrepidity – and he had filed teeth too, the poor devil, and the wool of his pate shaved into queer patterns, and three ornamental scars on each of his cheeks. He ought to have been clapping his hands and stamping his feet on the bank, instead of which he was hard at work, a thrall to strange witchcraft, full of improving knowledge. He was useful because he had been instructed; and what he knew was this – that should the water in that transparent thing disappear, the evil spirit inside the boiler would get angry through the greatness of his thirst, and take a terrible vengeance. So he sweated and fired up and watched the glass fearfully (with an impromptu charm, made of rags, tied to his arm, and a piece of polished bone, as big as a watch, stuck flatways through his lower lip), while the wooded banks slipped past us slowly, the short noise was left behind, the interminable miles of silence – and we crept on, towards Kurtz. But the snags were thick, the water was treacherous and shallow, the boiler seemed indeed to have a sulky devil in it, and thus neither that fireman nor I had any time to peer into our creepy thoughts.

'Some fifty miles below the Inner Station we came upon a hut of reeds, an inclined and melancholy pole, with the unrecognisable tatters of what had been a flag of some sort flying from it, and a neatly stacked wood-pile. This was unexpected. We came to the bank, and on the stack of firewood found a flat piece of board with some faded pencil-writing on it. When deciphered it said: "Wood for you. Hurry up. Approach cautiously." There was a signature, but it was illegible – not Kurtz – a much longer word. Hurry up. Where?

Up the river? "Approach cautiously." We had not done so. But the warning could not have been meant for the place where it could be only found after approach. Something was wrong above. But what – and how much? That was the question. We commented adversely upon the imbecility of that telegraphic style. The bush around said nothing, and would not let us look very far, either. A torn curtain of red twill hung in the doorway of the hut, and flapped sadly in our faces. The dwelling was dismantled; but we could see a white man had lived there not very long ago. There remained a rude table – a plank on two posts; a heap of rubbish reposed in a dark corner, and by the door I picked up a book. It had lost its covers, and the pages had been thumbed into a state of extremely dirty softness; but the back had been lovingly stitched afresh with white cotton thread, which looked clean yet. It was an extraordinary find. Its title was, "An Inquiry into some Points of Seamanship," by a man Tower, Towson – some such name[89] – Master in his Majesty's Navy. The matter looked dreary reading enough, with illustrative diagrams and repulsive tables of figures, and the copy was sixty years old. I handled this amazing antiquity with the greatest possible tenderness, lest it should dissolve in my hands. Within, Towson or Towser was inquiring earnestly into the breaking strain of ships' chains and tackle, and other such matters. Not a very enthralling book; but at the first glance you could see there a singleness of intention, an honest concern for the right way of going to work, which made these humble pages, thought out so many years ago, luminous with another than a professional light. The simple old sailor, with his talk of chains and purchases, made me forget the jungle and the pilgrims in a delicious sensation of having come upon something unmistakably real. Such a book being there was wonderful enough; but still more astounding were the notes pencilled in the margin, and plainly referring to the text. I couldn't believe my eyes! They were in cipher! Yes, it looked like cipher. Fancy a man lugging with him a book of that description into this nowhere and studying it – and making notes – in cipher at that! It was an extravagant mystery.

'I had been dimly aware for some time of a worrying noise, and when I lifted my eyes I saw the wood-pile was gone, and the manager, aided by all the pilgrims, was shouting at me from the river-side. I slipped the book into my pocket. I assure you to leave off reading was like tearing myself away from the shelter of an old and solid friendship.

'I started the lame engine ahead. "It must be this miserable trader – this intruder," exclaimed the manager, looking back malevolently at the place we had left. "He must be English," I said. "It will not save him from getting into trouble if he is not careful," muttered the manager darkly. I observed with assumed innocence that no man was safe from trouble in this world.

'The current was more rapid now, the steamer seemed at her last gasp, the stern-wheel flopped languidly, and I caught myself listening on tiptoe for the next beat of the float, for in sober truth I expected the wretched thing to give up every moment. It was like watching the last flickers of a life. But still we crawled. Sometimes I would pick out a tree a little way ahead to measure our progress towards Kurtz by, but I lost it invariably before we got abreast. To keep the eyes so long on one thing was too much for human patience. The manager displayed a beautiful resignation. I fretted and fumed and took to arguing with myself whether or no I would talk openly with Kurtz; but before I could come to any conclusion it occurred to me that my speech or my silence, indeed any action of mine, would be a mere futility. What did it matter what any one knew or ignored? What did it matter who was manager?

One gets sometimes such a flash of insight. The essentials of this affair lay deep under the surface, beyond my reach, and beyond my power of meddling.

'Towards the evening of the second day we judged ourselves about eight miles from Kurtz's station. I wanted to push on; but the manager looked grave, and told me the navigation up there was so dangerous that it would be advisable, the sun being very low already, to wait where we were till next morning. Moreover, he pointed out that if the warning to approach cautiously were to be followed, we must approach in daylight – not at dusk, or in the dark. This was sensible enough. Eight miles meant nearly three hours' steaming for us, and I could also see suspicious ripples at the upper end of the reach. Nevertheless, I was annoyed beyond expression at the delay, and most unreasonably too, since one night more could not matter much after so many months. As we had plenty of wood, and caution was the word, I brought up in the middle of the stream. The reach was narrow, straight, with high sides like a railway cutting. The dusk came gliding into it long before the sun had set. The current ran smooth and swift, but a dumb immobility sat on the banks. The living trees, lashed together by the creepers and every living bush of the undergrowth, might have been changed into stone, even to the slenderest twig, to the lightest leaf. It was not sleep – it seemed unnatural, like a state of trance.[90] Not the faintest sound of any kind could be heard. You looked on amazed, and began to suspect yourself of being deaf – then the night came suddenly, and struck you blind as well. About three in the morning some large fish leaped, and the loud splash made me jump as though a gun had been fired. When the sun rose there was a white fog, very warm and clammy, and more blinding than the night. It did not shift or drive; it was just there, standing all round you like something solid. At eight or nine, perhaps, it lifted as a shutter lifts. We had a glimpse of the towering multitude of trees, of the immense matted jungle, with the blazing little ball of the sun hanging over it – all perfectly still – and then the white shutter came down again, smoothly, as if sliding in greased grooves. I ordered the chain, which we had begun to heave in, to be paid out again. Before it stopped running with a muffled rattle, a cry, a very loud cry, as of infinite desolation, soared slowly in the opaque air. It ceased. A complaining clamour, modulated in savage discords, filled our ears. The sheer unexpectedness of it made my hair stir under my cap. I don't know how it struck the others: to me it seemed as though the mist itself had screamed, so suddenly, and apparently from all sides at once, did this tumultuous and mournful uproar arise. It culminated in a hurried outbreak of almost intolerably excessive shrieking, which stopped short, leaving us stiffened in a variety of silly attitudes, and obstinately listening to the nearly as appalling and excessive silence. "Good God! What is the meaning—?" stammered at my elbow one of the pilgrims, – a little fat man, with sandy hair and red whiskers, who wore side-spring boots, and pink pyjamas tucked into his socks. Two others remained open-mouthed a whole minute, then dashed into the little cabin, to rush out incontinently and stand darting scared glances, with Winchesters at "ready" in their hands. What we could see was just the steamer we were on, her outlines blurred as though she had been on the point of dissolving, and a misty strip of water, perhaps two feet broad, around her – and that was all. The rest of the world was nowhere, as far as our eyes and ears were concerned. Just nowhere. Gone, disappeared; swept off without leaving a whisper or a shadow behind.

'I went forward, and ordered the chain to be hauled in short, so as to be ready to trip the anchor and move the steamboat at once if necessary. "Will they attack?" whispered an awed voice. "We will all be butchered in this fog," murmured another. The faces twitched with the strain, the hands trembled slightly, the eyes forgot to wink. It was very curious to see the contrast of expressions of the white men and of the black fellows of our crew, who were as much strangers to that part of the river as we, though their homes were only eight hundred miles away.[91] The whites, of course greatly discomposed, had besides a curious look of being painfully shocked by such an outrageous row. The others had an alert, naturally interested expression; but their faces were essentially quiet, even those of the one or two who grinned as they hauled at the chain. Several exchanged short, grunting phrases, which seemed to settle the matter to their satisfaction. Their headman, a young, broad-chested black, severely draped in dark-blue fringed cloths, with fierce nostrils and his hair all done up artfully in oily ringlets, stood near me. "Aha!" I said, just for good fellowship's sake. "Catch 'im," he snapped, with a bloodshot widening of his eyes and a flash of sharp teeth – "catch 'im. Give 'im to us." "To you, eh?" I asked; "what would you do with them?" "Eat 'im!" he said, curtly, and, leaning his elbow on the rail, looked out into the fog in a dignified and profoundly pensive attitude. I would no doubt have been properly horrified, had it not occurred to me that he and his chaps must be very hungry: that they must have been growing increasingly hungry for at least this month past. They had been engaged for six months (I don't think a single one of them had any clear idea of time, as we at the end of countless ages have. They still belonged to the beginnings of time – had no inherited experience to teach them, as it were), and of course, as long as there was a piece of paper written over in accordance with some farcical law or other made down the river, it didn't enter anybody's head to trouble how they would live. Certainly they had brought with them some rotten hippo-meat, which couldn't have lasted very long, anyway, even if the pilgrims hadn't, in the midst of a shocking hulla-baloo, thrown a considerable quantity of it overboard. It looked like a high-handed proceeding; but it was really a case of legitimate self-defence. You can't breathe dead hippo waking, sleeping, and eating, and at the same time keep your precarious grip on existence. Besides that, they had given them every week three pieces of brass wire, each about nine inches long;[92] and the theory was they were to buy their provisions with that currency in river-side villages. You can see how *that* worked. There were either no villages, or the people were hostile, or the director, who like the rest of us fed out of tins, with an occasional old he-goat thrown in, didn't want to stop the steamer for some more or less recondite reason. So, unless they swallowed the wire itself, or made loops of it to snare the fishes with, I don't see what good their extravagant salary could be to them. I must say it was paid with a regularity worthy of a large and honourable trading company. For the rest, the only thing to eat – though it didn't look eatable in the least – I saw in their possession was a few lumps of some stuff like half-cooked dough,[93] of a dirty lavender colour, they kept wrapped in leaves, and now and then swallowed a piece of, but so small that it seemed done more for the looks of the thing than for any serious purpose of sustenance. Why in the name of all the gnawing devils of hunger they didn't go for us – they were thirty to five – and have a good tuck-in for once, amazes me now when I think of it. They were big powerful men, with not much capacity to weigh the consequences, with courage, with strength, even yet, though their skins were no longer glossy and their muscles no longer hard. And I saw that something restraining, one of those human secrets that baffle probability, had come into play there. I looked at them with a

swift quickening of interest – not because it occurred to me
I might be eaten by them before very long, though I own to
you that just then I perceived – in a new light, as it were –
how unwholesome the pilgrims looked, and I hoped, yes, I
positively hoped, that my aspect was not so – what shall I say?
– so – unappetising: a touch of fantastic vanity which fitted
well with the dream-sensation that pervaded all my days at
that time. Perhaps I had a little fever too. One can't live with
one's finger everlastingly on one's pulse. I had often "a little
fever," or a little touch of other things – the playful paw-
strokes of the wilderness, the preliminary trifling before the
more serious onslaught which came in due course. Yes; I
looked at them as you would on any human being, with a
curiosity of their impulses, motives, capacities, weaknesses,
when brought to the test of an inexorable physical necessity.
Restraint! What possible restraint? Was it superstition, disgust,
patience, fear – or some kind of primitive honour? No fear can
stand up to hunger, no patience can wear it out, disgust simply
does not exist where hunger is; and as to superstition, beliefs,
and what you may call principles, they are less than chaff in a
breeze. Don't you know the devilry of lingering starvation, its
exasperating torment, its black thoughts, its sombre and brooding ferocity? Well, I do. It takes a man all his inborn strength
to fight hunger properly. It's really easier to face bereavement,
dishonour, and the perdition of one's soul – than this kind of
prolonged hunger. Sad, but true. And these chaps too had no
earthly reason for any kind of scruple. Restraint! I would just
as soon have expected restraint from a hyena prowling amongst
the corpses of a battlefield. But there was the fact facing me –
the fact dazzling, to be seen, like the foam on the depths of the
sea, like a ripple on an unfathomable enigma, a mystery
greater – when I thought of it – than the curious, inexplicable
note of desperate grief in this savage clamour that had

swept by us on the river-bank, behind the blind whiteness of the fog.

'Two pilgrims were quarrelling in hurried whispers as to which bank. "Left." "No, no; how can you? Right, right, of course." "It is very serious," said the manager's voice behind me; "I would be desolated if anything should happen to Mr Kurtz before we came up." I looked at him, and had not the slightest doubt he was sincere. He was just the kind of man who would wish to preserve appearances. That was his restraint. But when he muttered something about going on at once, I did not even take the trouble to answer him. I knew, and he knew, that it was impossible. Were we to let go our hold of the bottom, we would be absolutely in the air – in space. We wouldn't be able to tell where we were going to – whether up or down stream, or across – till we fetched against one bank or the other, – and then we wouldn't know at first which it was. Of course I made no move. I had no mind for a smash-up. You couldn't imagine a more deadly place for a shipwreck. Whether drowned at once or not, we were sure to perish speedily in one way or another. "I authorise you to take all the risks," he said, after a short silence. "I refuse to take any," I said shortly; which was just the answer he expected, though its tone might have surprised him. "Well, I must defer to your judgment. You are captain," he said, with marked civility. I turned my shoulder to him in sign of my appreciation, and looked into the fog. How long would it last? It was the most hopeless look-out. The approach to this Kurtz grubbing for ivory in the wretched bush was beset by as many dangers as though he had been an enchanted princess sleeping in a fabulous castle.[94] "Will they attack, do you think?" asked the manager, in a confidential tone.

'I did not think they would attack, for several obvious reasons. The thick fog was one. If they left the bank in their canoes they would get lost in it, as we would be if we attempted to move. Still, I had also judged the jungle of both banks quite impenetrable – and yet eyes were in it, eyes that had seen us. The river-side bushes were certainly very thick; but the undergrowth behind was evidently penetrable. However, during the short lift I had seen no canoes anywhere in the reach – certainly not abreast of the steamer. But what made the idea of attack inconceivable to me was the nature of the noise – of the cries we had heard. They had not the fierce character boding of immediate hostile intention. Unexpected, wild, and violent as they had been, they had given me an irresistible impression of sorrow. The glimpse of the steamboat had for some reason filled those savages with unrestrained grief. The danger, if any, I expounded, was from our proximity to a great human passion let loose. Even extreme grief may ultimately vent itself in violence – but more generally takes the form of apathy. . . .

'You should have seen the pilgrims stare! They had no heart to grin, or even to revile me; but I believe they thought me gone mad – with fright, maybe. I delivered a regular lecture. My dear boys, it was no good bothering. Keep a look-out? Well, you may guess I watched the fog for the signs of lifting as a cat watches a mouse; but for anything else our eyes were of no more use to us than if we had been buried miles deep in a heap of cotton-wool. It felt like it too – choking, warm, stifling. Besides, all I said, though it sounded extravagant, was absolutely true to fact. What we afterwards alluded to as an attack was really an attempt at repulse. The action was very far from being aggressive – it was not even defensive, in the usual sense: it was undertaken under the stress of desperation, and in its essence was purely protective.

'It developed itself, I should say, two hours after the fog lifted, and its commencement was at a spot, roughly speaking, about a mile and a half below Kurtz's station. We had just floundered and flopped round a bend, when I saw an islet, a mere grassy hummock of bright green, in the middle of the stream. It was the only thing of the kind; but as we opened the reach more, I perceived it was the head of a long sandbank, or rather of a chain of shallow patches stretching down the middle of the river. They were discoloured, just awash, and the whole lot was seen just under the water, exactly as a man's backbone is seen running down the middle of his back under the skin. Now, as far as I did see, I could go to the right or to the left of this. I didn't know either channel, of course. The banks looked pretty well alike, the depth appeared the same; but as I had been informed the station was on the west side, I naturally headed for the western passage.

'No sooner had we fairly entered it than I became aware it was much narrower than I had supposed. To the left of us there was the long uninterrupted shoal, and to the right a high, steep bank heavily overgrown with bushes. Above the bush the trees stood in serried ranks. The twigs overhung the current thickly, and from distance to distance a large limb of some tree projected rigidly over the stream. It was then well on in the afternoon, the face of the forest was gloomy, and a broad strip of shadow had already fallen on the water. In this shadow we steamed up – very slowly, as you may imagine. I sheered her well inshore – the water being deepest near the bank, as the sounding-pole informed me.

'One of my hungry and forbearing friends was sounding in the bows just below me. This steamboat was exactly like a decked scow.[95] On the deck there were two little teak-wood houses, with doors and windows. The boiler was in the fore-end, and the machinery right astern. Over the whole there was a light roof, supported on stanchions. The funnel projected through that roof, and in front of the funnel a small cabin

74

built of light planks served for a pilot-house. It contained a couch, two camp-stools, a loaded Martini-Henry[96] leaning in one corner, a tiny table, and the steering-wheel. It had a wide door in front and a broad shutter at each side. All these were always thrown open, of course. I spent my days perched up there on the extreme fore-end of that roof, before the door. At night I slept, or tried to, on the couch. An athletic black belonging to some coast tribe, and educated by my poor predecessor, was the helmsman. He sported a pair of brass earrings, wore a blue cloth wrapper from the waist to the ankles, and thought all the world of himself. He was the most unstable kind of fool I had ever seen. He steered with no end of a swagger while you were by; but if he lost sight of you, he became instantly the prey of an abject funk, and would let that cripple of a steamboat get the upper hand of him in a minute.

'I was looking down at the sounding-pole, and feeling much annoyed to see at each try a little more of it stick out of that river, when I saw my poleman give up the business suddenly, and stretch himself flat on the deck, without even taking the trouble to haul his pole in. He kept hold on it though, and it trailed in the water. At the same time the fireman, whom I could also see below me, sat down abruptly before his furnace and ducked his head. I was amazed. Then I had to look at the river mighty quick, because there was a snag in the fairway. Sticks, little sticks, were flying about – thick: they were whizzing before my nose, dropping below me, striking behind me against my pilot-house. All this time the river, the shore, the woods, were very quiet – perfectly quiet. I could only hear the heavy splashing thump of the stern-wheel and the patter of these things. We cleared the snag clumsily. Arrows, by Jove! We were being shot at! I stepped in quickly to close the shutter on the landside. That fool-helmsman, his hands on the spokes, was lifting his knees high, stamping his feet, champing his mouth, like a reined-in horse. Confound him! And we were staggering within ten feet of the bank. I had to lean right out to swing the heavy shutter, and I saw a face amongst the leaves on the level with my own, looking at me very fierce and steady; and then suddenly, as though a veil had been removed from my eyes, I made out, deep in the tangled gloom, naked breasts, arms, legs, glaring eyes, – the bush was swarming with human limbs in movement, glistening, of bronze colour. The twigs shook, swayed, and rustled, the arrows flew out of them, and then the shutter came to. "Steer her straight," I said to the helmsman. He held his head rigid, face forward; but his eyes rolled, he kept on lifting and setting down his feet gently, his mouth foamed a little. "Keep quiet!" I said in a fury. I might just as well have ordered a tree not to sway in the wind. I darted out. Below me there was a great scuffle of feet on the iron deck; confused exclamations; a voice screamed, "Can you turn back?" I caught sight of a V-shaped ripple on the water ahead. What? Another snag! A fusillade burst out under my feet. The pilgrims had opened with their Winchesters, and were simply squirting lead into that bush. A deuce of a lot of smoke came up and drove slowly forward. I swore at it. Now I couldn't see the ripple or the snag either. I stood in the doorway, peering, and the arrows came in swarms. They might have been poisoned, but they looked as though they wouldn't kill a cat. The bush began to howl. Our wood-cutters raised a warlike whoop; the report of a rifle just at my back deafened me. I glanced over my shoulder, and the pilot-house was yet full of noise and smoke when I made a dash at the wheel. The fool-nigger had dropped everything, to throw the shutter open and let off that Martini-Henry. He stood before the wide opening, glaring, and I yelled at him to come back, while I straightened the sudden twist out of that steamboat. There was no room to turn even if I had wanted to, the snag was somewhere very near ahead in that confounded smoke, there was no time to lose, so I just crowded her into the bank – right into the bank, where I knew the water was deep.

'We tore slowly along the overhanging bushes in a whirl of broken twigs and flying leaves. The fusillade below stopped short, as I had foreseen it would when the squirts got empty. I threw my head back to a glinting whizz that traversed the pilot-house, in at one shutter-hole and out at the other. Looking past that mad helmsman, who was shaking the empty rifle and yelling at the shore, I saw vague forms of men running bent double, leaping, gliding, distinct, incomplete, evanescent. Something big appeared in the air before the shutter, the rifle went overboard, and the man stepped back swiftly, looked at me over his shoulder in an extraordinary, profound, familiar manner, and fell upon my feet. The side of his head hit the wheel twice, and the end of what appeared a long cane clattered round and knocked over a little camp-stool. It looked as though after wrenching that thing from somebody ashore he had lost his balance in the effort. The thin smoke had blown away, we were clear of the snag, and looking ahead I could see that in another hundred yards or so I would be free to sheer off, away from the bank; but my feet felt so very warm and wet that I had to look down. The man had rolled on his back and stared straight up at me; both his hands clutched that cane. It was the shaft of a spear that, either thrown or lunged through the opening, had caught him in the side just below the ribs; the blade had gone in out of sight, after making a frightful gash; my shoes were full; a pool of blood lay very still, gleaming dark-red under the wheel; his eyes shone with an amazing lustre. The fusillade burst out again. He looked at me anxiously, gripping the spear like something precious, with an air of being afraid I would try to take it away from him. I had to make an effort to free my eyes from his gaze and attend to the steering. With one hand I felt above my head for the line of the steam-whistle,[97] and jerked out screech after screech hurriedly. The tumult of angry and warlike yells was checked instantly, and then from the depths of the woods went out such a tremulous and prolonged wail of mournful fear and utter despair as may be imagined to follow the flight of the last hope from the earth. There was a great commotion in the bush; the shower of arrows stopped, a few dropping shots rang out sharply – then silence, in which the languid beat of the stern-wheel came plainly to my ears. I put the helm hard a-starboard at the moment when the pilgrim in pink pyjamas, very hot and agitated, appeared in the doorway. "The manager sends me—" he began in an official tone, and stopped short. "Good God!" he said, glaring at the wounded man.

'We two whites stood over him, and his lustrous and inquiring glance enveloped us both. I declare it looked as though he would presently put to us some question in an understandable language; but he died without uttering a sound, without moving a limb, without twitching a muscle. Only in the very last moment, as though in response to some sign we could not see, to some whisper we could not hear, he frowned heavily, and that frown gave to his black death-mask an inconceivably sombre, brooding, and menacing expression. The lustre of inquiring glance faded swiftly into vacant glassiness. "Can you steer?" I asked the agent eagerly. He looked very dubious; but I made a grab at his arm, and he understood at once I meant him to steer whether or no. To tell you the truth, I was morbidly anxious to change my shoes and socks. "He is dead," murmured the fellow, immensely impressed. "No doubt about it," said I, tugging like mad at the shoe-laces. "And, by the way, I suppose Mr Kurtz is dead as well by this time."

'For the moment that was the dominant thought. There was

a sense of extreme disappointment, as though I had found out I had been striving after something altogether without a substance. I couldn't have been more disgusted if I had travelled all this way for the sole purpose of talking with Mr Kurtz. Talking with ... I flung one shoe overboard, and became aware that that was exactly what I had been looking forward to – a talk with Kurtz. I made the strange discovery that I had never imagined him as doing, you know, but as discoursing. I didn't say to myself, "Now I will never see him," or "Now I will never shake him by the hand," but, "Now I will never hear him." The man presented himself as a voice. Not of course that I did not connect him with some sort of action. Hadn't I been told in all the tones of jealousy and admiration that he had collected, bartered, swindled, or stolen more ivory than all the other agents together. That was not the point. The point was in his being a gifted creature, and that of all his gifts the one that stood out pre-eminently, that carried with it a sense of real presence, was his ability to talk, his words – the gift of expression, the bewildering, the illuminating, the most exalted and the most contemptible, the pulsating stream of light, or the deceitful flow from the heart of an impenetrable darkness.

'The other shoe went flying unto the devil-god of that river. I thought, By Jove! it's all over. We are too late; he has vanished – the gift has vanished, by means of some spear, arrow, or club. I will never hear that chap speak after all, – and my sorrow had a startling extravagance of emotion, even such as I had noticed in the howling sorrow of these savages in the bush. I couldn't have felt more of lonely desolation somehow, had I been robbed of a belief or had missed my destiny in life. . . . Why do you sigh in this beastly way, somebody? Absurd? Well, absurd. Good Lord! mustn't a man ever— Here, give me some tobacco.' . . .

There was a pause of profound stillness, then a match flared, and Marlow's lean face appeared, worn, hollow, with downward folds and dropped eyelids, with an aspect of concentrated attention; and as he took vigorous draws at his pipe, it seemed to retreat and advance out of the night in the regular flicker of the tiny flame. The match went out.

'Absurd!' he cried. 'This is the worst of trying to tell ... Here you all are, each moored with two good addresses, like a hulk with two anchors, a butcher round one corner, a policeman round another, excellent appetites, and temperature normal – you hear – normal from year's end to year's end. And you say, Absurd! Absurd be – exploded! Absurd! My dear boys, what can you expect from a man who out of sheer nervousness had just flung overboard a pair of new shoes? Now I think of it, it is amazing I did not shed tears. I am, upon the whole, proud of my fortitude. I was cut to the quick at the idea of having lost the inestimable privilege of listening to the gifted Kurtz. Of course I was wrong. The privilege was waiting for me. Oh yes, I heard more than enough. And I was right, too. A voice. He was very little more than a voice. And I heard – him – it – this voice – other voices – all of them were so little more than voices – and the memory of that time itself lingers around me, impalpable, like a dying vibration of one immense jabber, silly, atrocious, sordid, savage, or simply mean, without any kind of sense. Voices, voices – even the girl herself – now—'

He was silent for a long time.

'I laid the ghost of his gifts at last with a lie,' he began suddenly. 'Girl! What? Did I mention a girl? Oh, she is out of it – completely. They – the women I mean – are out of it – should be out of it. We must help them to stay in that beautiful world of their own, lest ours gets worse. Oh, she had to be out of it. You should have heard the disinterred body of

Mr Kurtz saying, "My Intended." You would have perceived directly then how completely she was out of it. And the lofty frontal bone of Mr Kurtz! They say the hair goes on growing[98] sometimes, but this – ah – specimen was impressively bald. The wilderness had patted him on the head, and, behold, it was like a ball – an ivory ball; it had caressed him, and – lo! – he had withered; it had taken him, loved him, embraced him, got into his veins, consumed his flesh, and sealed his soul to its own by the inconceivable ceremonies of some devilish initiation. He was its spoiled and pampered favourite. Ivory? I should think so. Heaps of it, stacks of it. The old mud shanty was bursting with it. You would think there was not a single tusk left either above or below the ground in the whole country. "Mostly fossil," the manager had remarked disparagingly. It was no more fossil than I am; but they call it fossil when it is dug up. It appears these niggers do bury the tusks sometimes – but evidently they couldn't bury this parcel deep enough to save the gifted Mr Kurtz from his fate. We filled the steamboat with it, and had to pile a lot on the deck. Thus he could see and enjoy as long as he could see, because the appreciation of this favour had remained with him to the last. You should have heard him say, "My ivory." Oh yes, I heard him. "My Intended, my ivory, my station, my river, my—" everything belonged to him. It made me hold my breath in expectation of hearing the wilderness burst into a prodigious peal of laughter that would shake the fixed stars in their places. Everything belonged to him – but that was a trifle. The thing was to know what he belonged to, how many powers of darkness claimed him for their own. That was the reflection that made you creepy all over. It was impossible – it was not good for one either – trying to imagine. He had taken a high seat amongst the devils of the land – I mean literally. You can't understand. How could you? – with solid pavement under your feet, surrounded by kind neighbours ready to cheer you or to fall on you, stepping delicately between the butcher and the policeman, in the holy terror of scandal and gallows and lunatic asylums – how can you imagine what particular region of the first ages a man's untrammelled feet may take him into by the way of solitude – utter solitude without a policeman – by the way of silence – utter silence, where no warning voice of a kind neighbour can be heard whispering of public opinion? These little things make all the great difference. When they are gone you must fall back upon your own innate strength, upon your own capacity for faithfulness. Of course you may be too much of a fool to go wrong – too dull even to know you are being assaulted by the powers of darkness. I take it, no fool ever made a bargain for his soul with the devil: the fool is too much of a fool, or the devil too much of a devil – I don't know which. Or you may be such a thunderingly exalted creature as to be altogether deaf and blind to anything but heavenly sights and sounds. Then the earth for you is only a standing place – and whether to be like this is your loss or your gain I won't pretend to say. But most of us are neither one nor the other. The earth for us is a place to live in, where we must put up with sights, with sounds, with smells too, by Jove! – breathe dead hippo, so to speak, and not be contaminated. And there, don't you see? your strength comes in, the faith in your ability for the digging of unostentatious holes to bury the stuff in – your power of devotion, not to yourself, but to an obscure, back-breaking business. And that's difficult enough. Mind, I am not trying to excuse or even explain – I am trying to account to myself for – for – Mr Kurtz – for the shade of Mr Kurtz. This initiated wraith from the back of Nowhere honoured me with its amazing confidence before it vanished altogether. This was because it could speak English to me. The original Kurtz had been educated partly in England, and – as he was good enough to say himself – his sympathies were in the right place. His mother was half-English, his father was half-French.[99] All Europe contributed to the making of Kurtz; and by-and-by I learned that, most appropriately, the International Society for the Suppression of Savage Customs[100] had intrusted him with the making of a report, for its future guidance. And he had written it too. I've seen it. I've read it. It was eloquent, vibrating with eloquence, but too high-strung, I think. Seventeen pages of close writing he had found time for! But this must have been before his – let us say – nerves went wrong, and caused him to preside at certain midnight dances ending with unspeakable rites, which – as far as I reluctantly gathered from what I heard at various times – were offered up to him – do you understand? – to Mr Kurtz himself. But it was a beautiful piece of writing. The opening paragraph, however, in the light of later information, strikes me now as ominous. He began with the argument that we whites, from the point of development we had arrived at, "must necessarily appear to them [savages] in the nature of supernatural beings – we approach them with the might as of a deity," and so on, and so on. "By the simple exercise of our will we can exert a power for good practically unbounded," &c., &c. From that point he soared and took me with him. The peroration was magnificent, though difficult to remember, you know. It gave me the notion of an exotic Immensity ruled by an august Benevolence. It made me tingle with enthusiasm. This was the unbounded power of eloquence – of words – of burning noble words. There were no practical hints to interrupt the magic current of phrases, unless a kind of note at the foot of the last page, scrawled evidently much later, in an unsteady hand, may be regarded as the exposition of a method. It was very simple, and at the end of that moving appeal to every altruistic sentiment it blazed at you, luminous and terrifying, like a flash of lightning in a serene sky: "Exterminate all the brutes!" The curious part was that he had apparently forgotten all about that valuable postscriptum, because, later on, when he in a sense came to himself, he repeatedly entreated me to take good care of "my pamphlet" (he called it), as it was sure to have in the future a good influence upon his career. I had full information about all these things, and, besides, as it turned out, I was to have the care of his memory. I've done enough for it to give me the indisputable right to lay it, if I choose, for an everlasting rest in the dust-bin of progress, amongst all the sweepings and, figuratively speaking, all the dead cats of civilisation. But then, you see, I can't choose. He won't be forgotten. Whatever he was, he was not common. He had the power to charm or frighten rudimentary souls into an aggravated witch-dance in his honour; he could also fill the small souls of the pilgrims with bitter misgivings: he had one devoted friend at least, and he had conquered one soul in the world that was neither rudimentary nor tainted with self-seeking. No; I can't forget him, though I am not prepared to affirm the fellow was exactly worth the life we lost in getting to him. I missed my late helmsman awfully, – I missed him even while his body was still lying in the pilot-house. Perhaps you will think it passing strange this regret for a savage who was no more account than a grain of sand in a black Sahara. Well, don't you see, he had done something, he had steered; for months I had him at my back – a help – an instrument. It was a kind of partnership. He steered for me – I had to look after him, I worried about his deficiencies, and thus a subtle bond had been created, of which I only became aware when it was suddenly broken. And the intimate profundity of that look he gave me when he received his hurt remains to this day in my memory – like a claim of distant kinship affirmed in a supreme moment.

'Poor fool! If he had only left that shutter alone. He had no restraint, no restraint – just like Kurtz – a tree swayed by the wind. As soon as I had put on a dry pair of slippers, I dragged him out, after first jerking the spear out of his side, which operation I confess I performed with my eyes shut tight. His heels leaped together over the little doorstep; his shoulders were pressed to my breast; I hugged him from behind desperately. Oh! he was heavy, heavy; heavier than any man on earth, I should imagine. Then without more ado I tipped him overboard. The current snatched him as though he had been a wisp of grass, and I saw the body roll over twice before I lost sight of it for ever. All the pilgrims and the manager were then congregated on the awning-deck about the pilot-house, chattering at each other like a flock of excited magpies, and there was a scandalised murmur at my heartless promptitude. What they wanted to keep that body hanging about for I can't guess. Embalm it, maybe. But I had also heard another, and a very ominous, murmur on the deck below. My friends the woodcutters were likewise scandalised, and with a better show of reason – though I admit that the reason itself was quite inadmissible. Oh, quite! I had made up my mind that if my late helmsman was to be eaten, the fishes alone should have him. He had been a very second-rate helmsman while alive, but now he was dead he might have become a first-class temptation, and possibly cause some startling trouble. Besides, I was anxious to take the wheel, the man in pink pyjamas showing himself a hopeless duffer at the business.

'This I did directly the simple funeral was over. We were going half-speed, keeping right in the middle of the stream, and I listened to the talk about me. They had given up Kurtz, they had given up the station; Kurtz was dead, and the station

had been burnt – and so on – and so on. The red-haired
pilgrim was beside himself with the thought that at least this
poor Kurtz had been properly revenged. "Say! We must have
made a glorious slaughter of them in the bush. Eh? What do
you think? Say?" He positively danced, the bloodthirsty little
gingery beggar. And he had nearly fainted when he saw the
wounded man! I could not help saying, "You made a glorious
lot of smoke, anyhow." I had seen, from the way the tops of
the bushes rustled and flew, that almost all the shots had gone
too high. You can't hit anything unless you take aim and fire
from the shoulder; but these chaps fired from the hip with
their eyes shut. The retreat, I maintained – and I was right –
was caused by the screeching of the steam-whistle. Upon this
they forgot Kurtz, and began to howl at me with indignant
protests.

'The manager stood by the wheel murmuring confidentially
about the necessity of getting well away down the river before
dark at all events, when I saw in the distance a clearing on the
river-side and the outlines of some sort of building. "What's
this?" I asked. He clapped his hands in wonder. "The station!"
he cried. I edged in at once, still going half-speed.

'Through my glasses I saw the slope of a hill interspersed
with rare trees and perfectly free from undergrowth. A long
decaying building on the summit was half buried in the high
grass; the large holes in the peaked roof gaped black from afar;
the jungle and the woods made a background. There was no
enclosure or fence of any kind; but there had been one
apparently, for near the house half-a-dozen slim posts remained
in a row, roughly trimmed, and with their upper ends orna-
mented with round carved balls. The rails, or whatever there
had been between, had disappeared. Of course the forest
surrounded all that. The river-bank was clear, and on the
waterside I saw a white man under a hat like a cart-wheel

beckoning persistently with his whole arm. Examining the edge of the forest above and below, I was almost certain I could see movements – human forms gliding here and there. I steamed past prudently, then stopped the engines and let her drift down. The man on the shore began to shout, urging us to land. "We have been attacked," screamed the manager. "I know – I know. It's all right," yelled back the other, as cheerful as you please. "Come along. It's all right. I am glad."

'His aspect reminded me of something I had seen – something funny I had seen somewhere. As I manœuvred to get alongside, I was asking myself, "What does this fellow look like?" Suddenly I got it. He looked like a harlequin.[101] His clothes had been made of some stuff that was brown holland probably, but it was covered with patches all over, with bright patches, blue, red, and yellow,[102] – patches on the back, patches on front, patches on elbows, on knees; coloured binding round his jacket, scarlet edging at the bottom of his trousers; and the sunshine made him look extremely gay and wonderfully neat withal, because you could see how beautifully all this patching had been done. A beardless, boyish face, very fair, no features to speak of, nose peeling, little blue eyes, smiles and frowns chasing each other over that open countenance like sunshine and shadow on a wind-swept plain. "Look out, captain!" he cried; "there's a snag lodged in here last night." What! Another snag? I confess I swore shamefully. I had nearly holed my cripple, to finish off that charming trip. The harlequin on the bank turned his little pug nose up to me. "You English?" he asked, all smiles. "Are you?" I shouted from the wheel. The smiles vanished, and he shook his head as if sorry for my disappointment. Then he brightened up. "Never mind!" he cried encouragingly. "Are we in time?" I asked. "He is up there," he replied, with a toss of the head up the hill, and becoming gloomy all of a sudden. His face was like the autumn sky, overcast one moment and bright the next.

'When the manager, escorted by the pilgrims, all of them armed to the teeth, had gone to the house, this chap came on board. "I say, I don't like this. These natives are in the bush," I said. He assured me earnestly it was all right. "They are simple people," he added; "well, I am glad you came. It took me all my time to keep them off." "But you said it was all right," I cried. "Oh, they meant no harm," he said; and as I stared he corrected himself, "Not exactly." Then vivaciously, "My faith, your pilot-house wants a clean-up!" In the next breath he advised me to keep enough steam on the boiler to blow the whistle in case of any trouble. "One good screech will do more for you than all your rifles. They are simple people," he repeated. He rattled away at such a rate he quite overwhelmed me. He seemed to be trying to make up for lots of silence, and actually hinted, laughing, that such was the case. "Don't you talk with Mr Kurtz?" I said. "You don't talk with that man – you listen to him," he exclaimed with severe exaltation. "But now—" He waved his arm, and in the twinkling of an eye was in the uttermost depths of despondency. In a moment he came up again with a jump, possessed himself of both my hands, shook them continuously, while he gabbled: "Brother sailor . . . honour . . . pleasure . . . delight . . . introduce myself . . . Russian . . . son of an arch-priest . . . Government of Tambov[103] . . . What? Tobacco! English tobacco; the excellent English tobacco! Now, that's brotherly. Smoke? Where's a sailor that does not smoke?"

'The pipe soothed him, and gradually I made out he had run away from school, had gone to sea in a Russian ship; ran away again; served some time in English ships; was now reconciled with the arch-priest. He made a point of that. "But when one is young one must see things, gather experience, ideas; enlarge the mind." "Here!" I interrupted. "You can never tell! Here I have met Mr Kurtz," he said, youthfully solemn and reproachful. I held my tongue after that. It appears he had persuaded a Dutch trading-house on the coast[104] to fit him out with stores and goods, and had started for the interior with a light heart, and no more idea of what would happen to him than a baby. He had been wandering about that river for nearly two years alone, cut off from everybody and everything. "I am not so young as I look. I am twenty-five," he said. "At first old Van Shuyten[105] would tell me to go to the devil," he narrated with keen enjoyment; "but I stuck to him, and talked and talked, till at last he got afraid I would talk the hind-leg off his favourite dog, so he gave me some cheap things and a few guns, and told me he hoped he would never see my face again. Good old Dutchman, Van Shuyten. I sent him one small lot of ivory a year ago, so that he can't call me a little thief when I get back. I hope he got it. And for the rest, I don't care. I had some wood stacked for you. That was my old house. Did you see?"

'I gave him Towson's book. He made as though he would kiss me, but restrained himself. "The only book I had left, and I thought I had lost it," he said, looking at it ecstatically. "So many accidents happen to a man going about alone, you know. Canoes get upset sometimes – and sometimes you've got to clear out so quick when the people get angry." He thumbed the pages. "You made notes in Russian?" I asked. He nodded. "I thought they were written in cipher," I said. He laughed, then became serious. "I had lots of trouble to keep these people off," he said. "Did they want to kill you?" I asked. "Oh no!" he cried, and checked himself. "Why did they attack us?" I pursued. He hesitated, then said shamefacedly, "They don't want him to go." "Don't they?" I said, curiously. He nodded a nod full of mystery and wisdom. "I tell you," he cried, "this man has enlarged my mind." He opened his arms wide, staring at me with his little blue eyes that were perfectly round.'

3

'I looked at him, lost in astonishment. There he was before me, in motley, as though he had absconded from a troupe of mimes, enthusiastic, fabulous. His very existence was improbable, inexplicable, and altogether bewildering. He was an insoluble problem. It was inconceivable how he had existed, how he had succeeded in getting so far, how he had managed to remain – why he did not instantly disappear. "I went a little farther," he said, "then still a little farther – till I had gone so far that I don't know how I'll ever get back. Never mind. Plenty time. I can manage. You take Kurtz away quick – quick – I tell you." The glamour of youth enveloped his particoloured rags, his destitution, his loneliness, the essential desolation of his futile wanderings. For months – for years – his life hadn't been worth a day's purchase; and there he was gallantly, thoughtlessly alive, to all appearance indestructible solely by the virtue of his few years and of his unreflecting audacity. I was seduced into something like admiration – like envy. Glamour urged him on, glamour kept him unscathed. He surely wanted nothing from the wilderness but space to breathe in and to push on through. His need was to exist, and to move onwards at the greatest possible risk, and with a maximum of privation. If the absolutely pure, uncalculating, unpractical spirit of adventure had ever ruled a human being, it ruled this be-patched youth. I almost envied him the possession of this modest and clear flame. It seemed to have consumed all thought of self so completely, that, even while he was talking to you, you forgot that it was he – the man before your eyes – who had gone through these things. I did not envy him his devotion to Kurtz, though. He had not meditated over it. It came to him, and he accepted it with a sort of eager fatalism. I must say that to me it appeared about the most dangerous thing in every way he had come upon so far.

'They had come together unavoidably, like two ships be-calmed near each other, and lay rubbing sides at last. I suppose Kurtz wanted an audience, because on a certain occasion, when encamped in the forest, they had talked all night, or more probably Kurtz had talked. "We talked of everything," he said, quite transported at the recollection. "I forgot there was such a thing as sleep. The night did not seem to last an hour. Everything! Everything! . . . Of love too." "Ah, he talked to you of love!" I said, much amused. "It isn't what you think," he cried, almost passionately. "It was in general. He made me see things – things."

'He threw his arms up. We were on deck at the time, and the headman of my wood-cutters, lounging near by, turned upon him his heavy and glittering eyes. I looked around, and I don't know why, but I assure you that never, never before, did this land, this river, this jungle, the very arch of this blazing sky, appear to me so hopeless and so dark, so impenetrable to human thought, so pitiless to human weakness. "And, ever since, you have been with him, of course?" I said.

'On the contrary. It appears their intercourse had been very much broken by various causes. He had, as he informed me proudly, managed to nurse Kurtz through two illnesses (he alluded to it as you would to some risky feat), but as a rule Kurtz wandered alone, far in the depths of the forest. "Very often coming to this station, I had to wait days and days before he would turn up," he said. "Ah, it was worth waiting for! – sometimes." "What was he doing? exploring or what?" I asked. "Oh yes, of course"; he had discovered lots of villages, a lake too – he did not know exactly in what direction; it was dangerous to inquire too much – but mostly his expeditions had been for ivory. "But he had no goods to trade with by that time," I objected. "There's a good lot of cartridges left even yet," he answered, looking away. "To speak plainly, he raided the country," I said. He nodded. "Not alone, surely!" He muttered something about the villages round that lake. "Kurtz got the tribe to follow him, did he?" I suggested. He fidgeted a little. "They adored him," he said. The tone of these words was so extraordinary that I looked at him searchingly. It was curious to see his mingled eagerness and reluctance to speak of Kurtz. The man filled his life, occupied his thoughts, swayed his emotions. "What can you expect?" he burst out; "he came to them with thunder and lightning, you know – and they had never seen anything like it – and very terrible. He could be very terrible. You can't judge Mr Kurtz as you would an ordinary man. No, no, no! Now – just to give you an idea – I don't mind telling you, he wanted to shoot me too one day – but I don't judge him." "Shoot you!" I cried. "What for?" "Well, I had a small lot of ivory the chief of that village near my house gave me. You see I used to shoot game for them. Well, he wanted it, and wouldn't hear reason. He declared he would shoot me unless I gave him the ivory and then cleared out of the country, because he could do so, and had a fancy for it, and there was nothing on earth to prevent him killing whom he jolly well pleased. And it was true too. I gave him the ivory. What did I care! But I didn't clear out. No, no. I couldn't leave him. I had to be careful, of course, till we got friendly again for a time. He had his second illness then.

Afterwards I had to keep out of the way; but I didn't mind. He was living for the most part in those villages on the lake. When he came down to the river, sometimes he would take to me, and sometimes it was better for me to be careful. This man suffered too much. He hated all this, and somehow he couldn't get away. When I had a chance I begged him to try and leave while there was time; I offered to go back with him. And he would say yes, and then he would remain; go off on another ivory hunt; disappear for weeks; forget himself amongst these people – forget himself – you know." "Why! he's mad," I said. He protested indignantly. Mr Kurtz couldn't be mad. If I had heard him talk, only two days ago, I wouldn't dare hint at such a thing. . . . I had taken up my binoculars while we talked, and was looking at the shore, sweeping the limit of the forest at each side and at the back of the house. The consciousness of there being people in that bush, so silent, so quiet – as silent and quiet as the ruined house on the hill – made me uneasy. There was no sign on the face of nature of this amazing tale that was not so much told as suggested to me in desolate exclamations, completed by shrugs, in interrupted phrases, in hints ending in deep sighs. The woods were unmoved, like a mask – heavy, like the closed door of a prison – they looked with their air of hidden knowledge, of patient expectation, of unapproachable silence. The Russian was explaining to me that it was only lately that Mr Kurtz had come down to the river, bringing along with him all the fighting men of that lake tribe. He had been absent for several months – getting himself adored, I suppose – and had come down unexpectedly, with the intention to all appearance of making a raid either across the river or down stream. Evidently the appetite for more ivory had got the better of the – what shall I say? – less material aspirations. However, he had got much worse suddenly. "I heard he was lying helpless, and so I came up – took my chance," said the Russian. "Oh, he is bad, very bad." I directed my glass to the house. There were no signs of life, but there was the ruined roof, the long mud wall peeping above the grass, with three little square window-holes, no two of the same size; all this brought within reach of my hand, as it were. And then I made a brusque movement, and one of the remaining posts of that vanished fence leaped up in the field of my glass. You remember I told you I had been struck at the distance by certain attempts at ornamentation, rather remarkable in the ruinous aspect of the place. Now I had suddenly a nearer view, and its first result was to make me throw my head back as if before a blow. Then I went carefully from post to post with my glass, and I saw my mistake. These round knobs were not ornamental but symbolic; they were expressive and puzzling, striking and disturbing – food for thought and also for the vultures if there had been any looking down from the sky; but at all events for such ants as were industrious enough to ascend the pole. They would have been even more impressive, those heads on the stakes,[106] if their faces had not been turned to the house. Only one, the first I had made out, was facing my way. I was not so shocked as you may think. The start back I had given was really nothing but a movement of surprise. I had expected to see a knob of wood there, you know. I returned deliberately to the first I had seen – and there it was, black, dried, sunken, with closed eyelids, – a head that seemed to sleep at the top of that pole, and, with the shrunken dry lips showing a narrow white line of the teeth, was smiling too, smiling continuously at some endless and jocose dream of that eternal slumber.

'I am not disclosing any trade secrets. In fact the manager said afterwards that Mr Kurtz's methods had ruined the district. I have no opinion on that point, but I want you clearly to understand that there was nothing exactly profitable in these heads being there. They only showed that Mr Kurtz lacked restraint in the gratification of his various lusts, that there was something wanting in him – some small matter which, when the pressing need arose, could not be found under his magnificent eloquence. Whether he knew of this deficiency himself I can't say. I think the knowledge came to him at last – only at the very last. But the wilderness had found him out early, and had taken on him a terrible vengeance for the fantastic invasion. I think it had whispered to him things about himself which he did not know, things of which he had no conception till he took counsel with this great solitude – and the whisper had proved irresistibly fascinating. It echoed loudly within him because he was hollow at the core. . . . I put down the glass, and the head that had appeared near enough to be spoken to seemed at once to have leaped away from me into inaccessible distance.

'The admirer of Mr Kurtz was a bit crestfallen. In a hurried, indistinct voice he began to assure me he had not dared to take these – say, symbols – down. He was not afraid of the natives; they would not stir till Mr Kurtz gave the word. His ascendancy was extraordinary. The camps of these people surrounded the place, and the chiefs came every day to see him. They would crawl . . . "I don't want to know anything of the ceremonies used when approaching Mr Kurtz," I shouted. Curious, this feeling that came over me that such details would be more intolerable than those heads drying on the stakes under Mr Kurtz's windows. After all, that was only a savage sight, while I seemed at one bound to have been transported into some lightless region of subtle horrors, where pure, uncomplicated savagery was a positive relief, being something that had a right to exist – obviously – in the sunshine. The young man looked at me with surprise. I suppose it did not occur to him Mr Kurtz was no idol of mine. He forgot I hadn't heard any of these splendid monologues on, what was it? on love, justice, conduct of life – or what not. If it had come to crawling before Mr Kurtz, he crawled as much as the veriest savage of them all. I had no idea of the conditions, he said: these heads were the heads of rebels. I shocked him excessively by laughing. Rebels! What would be the next definition I was to hear? There had been enemies, criminals, workers – and these were rebels. Those rebellious heads looked very subdued to me on their sticks. "You don't know how such a life tries a man like Kurtz," cried Kurtz's last disciple. "Well, and you?" I said. "I! I! I am a simple man. I have no great thoughts. I want nothing from anybody. How can you compare me to . . .?" His feelings were too much for speech, and suddenly he broke down. "I don't understand," he groaned. "I've been doing my best to keep him alive, and that's enough. I had no hand in all this. I have no abilities. There hasn't been a drop of medicine or a mouthful of invalid food for months here. He was shamefully abandoned. A man like this, with such ideas. Shamefully! Shamefully! I – I – haven't slept for the last ten nights. . . ."

'His voice lost itself in the calm of the evening. The long shadows of the forest had slipped down-hill while we talked, had gone far beyond the ruined hovel, beyond the symbolic row of stakes. All this was in the gloom, while we down there were yet in the sunshine, and the stretch of the river abreast of the clearing glittered in a still and dazzling splendour, with a murky and overshadowed bend above and below. Not a living soul was seen on the shore. The bushes did not rustle.

'Suddenly round the corner of the house a group of men appeared, as though they had come up from the ground. They waded waist-deep in the grass, in a compact body, bearing an improvised stretcher in their midst. Instantly, in the emptiness of the landscape, a cry arose whose shrillness pierced the still air like a sharp arrow flying straight to the very heart of the land; and, as if by enchantment, streams of human beings – of naked human beings – with spears in their hands, with bows, with shields, with wild glances and savage movements, were poured into the clearing by the dark-faced and pensive forest. The bushes shook, the grass swayed for a time, and then everything stood still in attentive immobility.

'"Now, if he does not say the right thing to them we are all done for," said the Russian at my elbow. The knot of men with the stretcher had stopped too, half-way to the steamer, as if petrified. I saw the man on the stretcher sit up, lank and with an uplifted arm, above the shoulders of the bearers. "Let us hope that the man who can talk so well of love in general will find some particular reason to spare us this time," I said. I resented bitterly the absurd danger of our situation, as if to be at the mercy of that atrocious phantom had been a dishonouring necessity. I could not hear a sound, but through my glasses I saw the thin arm extended commandingly, the lower jaw moving, the eyes of that apparition shining darkly far in its bony head that nodded with grotesque jerks. Kurtz – Kurtz – that means "short" in German – don't it? Well, the name was as true as everything else in his life – and death. He looked at least seven feet long. His covering had fallen off, and his body emerged from it pitiful and appalling as from a winding-sheet. I could see the cage of his ribs all astir, the bones of his arm waving. It was as though an animated image of death carved out of old ivory had been shaking its hand with menaces at a motionless crowd of men made of dark and glittering bronze. I saw him open his mouth wide – it gave him a weirdly voracious aspect, as though he had wanted to swallow all the air, all the earth, all the men before him. A deep voice reached me faintly. He must have been shouting. He fell back suddenly. The stretcher shook as the bearers staggered forward again, and almost at the same time I noticed that the crowd of savages was vanishing without any perceptible movement of retreat, as if the forest that had ejected these beings so suddenly had drawn them in again as the breath is drawn in a long aspiration.

'Some of the pilgrims behind the stretcher carried his arms – two shot-guns, a heavy rifle, and a light revolver-carbine – the thunderbolts of that pitiful Jupiter. The manager bent over him murmuring as he walked beside his head. They laid him down in one of the little cabins – just a room for a bed-place and a camp-stool or two, you know. We had brought his belated correspondence, and a lot of torn envelopes and open letters littered his bed. His hand roamed feebly amongst these papers. I was struck by the fire of his eyes and the composed languor of his expression. It was not so much the exhaustion of disease. He did not seem in pain. This shadow looked satiated and calm, as though for the moment it had had its fill of all the emotions.

'He rustled one of the letters, and looking straight in my face said, "I am glad." Somebody had been writing to him about me. These special recommendations were turning up again. The volume of tone he emitted without effort, almost without the trouble of moving his lips, amazed me. A voice! a voice! It was grave, profound, vibrating, while the man did not seem capable of a whisper. However, he had enough strength in him – factitious no doubt – to very nearly make an end of us, as you shall hear directly.

'The manager appeared silently in the doorway; I stepped out at once and he drew the curtain after me. The Russian, eyed curiously by the pilgrims, was staring at the shore. I followed the direction of his glance.

'Dark human shapes could be made out in the distance, flitting indistinctly against the gloomy border of the forest, and near the river two bronze figures, leaning on tall spears, stood in the sunlight under fantastic head-dresses of spotted skins, warlike and still in statuesque repose. And from right to left along the lighted shore moved a wild and gorgeous apparition of a woman.

'She walked with measured steps, draped in striped and fringed cloths, treading the earth proudly, with a slight jingle and flash of barbarous ornaments. She carried her head high; her hair was done in the shape of a helmet; she had brass leggings to the knee, brass wire gauntlets to the elbow, a crimson spot on her tawny cheek, innumerable necklaces of glass beads on her neck; bizarre things, charms, gifts of witch-men, that hung about her, glittered and trembled at every step. She must have had the value of several elephant tusks upon her. She was savage and superb, wild-eyed and magnificent; there was something ominous and stately in her deliberate progress. And in the hush that had fallen suddenly upon the whole sorrowful land, the immense wilderness, the colossal body of the fecund and mysterious life seemed to look at her, pensive, as though it had been looking at the image of its own tenebrous and passionate soul.

'She came abreast of the steamer, stood still, and faced us. Her long shadow fell to the water's edge. Her face had a tragic and fierce aspect of wild sorrow and of dumb pain mingled with the fear of some struggling, half-shaped resolve. She stood looking at us without a stir, and like the wilderness itself, with an air of brooding over an inscrutable purpose. A whole minute passed, and then she made a step forward. There was a low jingle, a glint of yellow metal, a sway of fringed draperies, and she stopped as if her heart had failed her. The young fellow by my side growled. The pilgrims murmured at my back. She looked at us all as if her life had depended upon the unswerving steadiness of her glance.

Suddenly she opened her bared arms and threw them up rigid above her head, as though in an uncontrollable desire to touch the sky, and at the same time the swift shadows darted out on the earth, swept around on the river, gathering the steamer in a shadowy embrace. A formidable silence hung over the scene.

'She turned away slowly, walked on, following the bank, and passed into the bushes to the left. Once only her eyes gleamed back at us in the dusk of the thickets before she disappeared.

'"If she had offered to come aboard I really think I would have tried to shoot her," said the man of patches, nervously. "I had been risking my life every day for the last fortnight to keep her out of the house. She got in one day and kicked up a row about those miserable rags I picked up in the storeroom to mend my clothes with. I wasn't decent. At least it must have been that, for she talked like a fury to Kurtz for an hour, pointing at me now and then. I don't understand the dialect of this tribe. Luckily for me, I fancy Kurtz felt too ill that day to care, or there would have been mischief. I don't understand. . . . No – it's too much for me. Ah, well, it's all over now."

'At this moment I heard Kurtz's deep voice behind the curtain, "Save me! – save the ivory, you mean. Don't tell me. Save *me*! Why, I've had to save you. You are interrupting my plans now. Sick! Sick! Not so sick as you would like to believe. Never mind. I'll carry my ideas out yet – I will return. I'll show you what can be done. You with your little peddling notions – you are interfering with me. I will return. I . . ."

'The manager came out. He did me the honour to take me under the arm and lead me aside. "He is very low, very low," he said. He considered it necessary to sigh, but neglected to be consistently sorrowful. "We have done all we could for him – haven't we? But there is no disguising the fact, Mr Kurtz has done more harm than good to the Company. He did not see the time was not ripe for vigorous action. Cautiously, cautiously – that's my principle. We must be cautious yet. The district is closed to us for a time. Deplorable! Upon the whole, the trade will suffer. I don't deny there is a remarkable quantity of ivory – mostly fossil.[107] We must save it, at all events – but look how precarious the position is – and why? Because the method is unsound." "Do you," said I, looking at the shore, "call it 'unsound method'?" "Without doubt," he exclaimed, hotly. "Don't you?" . . . "No method at all," I murmured after a while. "Exactly," he exulted. "I anticipated this. Shows a complete want of judgment. It is my duty to point it out in the proper quarter." "Oh," said I, "that fellow – what's his name? – the brickmaker, will make a readable report for you." He appeared confounded for a moment. It seemed to me I had never breathed an atmosphere so vile, and I turned mentally to Kurtz for relief – positively for relief. "Nevertheless, I think Mr Kurtz is a remarkable man," I said with emphasis. He started, dropped on me a cold heavy glance, said very quietly, "He *was*," and turned his back on me. My hour of favour was over; I found myself lumped along with Kurtz as a partisan of methods for which the time was not ripe: I was unsound! Ah! but it was something to have at least a choice of nightmares.

'I had turned to the wilderness really, not to Mr Kurtz, who, I was ready to admit, was as good as buried. And for a moment it seemed to me as if I also were buried in a vast grave full of unspeakable secrets. I felt an intolerable weight oppressing my breast, the smell of the damp earth, the unseen presence of victorious corruption, the darkness of an impenetrable night. . . . The Russian tapped me on the shoulder. I heard him mumbling and stammering something about "brother seaman – couldn't conceal – knowledge of matters that would affect Mr Kurtz's reputation." I waited. For him evidently Mr Kurtz was not in his grave; I suspect that for him Mr Kurtz was one of the immortals. "Well!" said I at last, "speak out. As it happens, I am Mr Kurtz's friend – in a way."

'He stated with a good deal of formality that had we not been "of the same profession," he would have kept the matter to himself without regard to consequences. He suspected "there was an active ill-will towards him on the part of these white men that—" "You are right," I said, remembering a certain conversation I had overheard. "The manager thinks you ought to be hanged." He showed a concern at this intelligence which amused me at first. "I had better get out of the way quietly," he said, earnestly. "I can do no more for Kurtz now, and they would soon find some excuse. What's to stop them? There's a military post three hundred miles from here." "Well, upon my word," said I, "perhaps you had better go if you have any friends amongst the savages near by." "Plenty," he said. "They are simple people – and I want nothing, you know." He stood biting his lip, then: "I don't want any harm to happen to these whites here, but of course I was thinking of Mr Kurtz's reputation – but you are a brother seaman and—" "All right," said I, after a time. "Mr Kurtz's reputation is safe with me." I did not know how truly I spoke.

'He informed me, lowering his voice, that it was Kurtz who had ordered the attack to be made on the steamer. "He hated sometimes the idea of being taken away – and then again . . . But I don't understand these matters. I am a simple man. He thought it would scare you away – that you would give it up, thinking him dead. I could not stop him. Oh, I had an awful time of it this last month." "Very well," I said. "He is all right now." "Ye-e-es," he muttered, not very convinced apparently. "Thanks," said I; "I shall keep my eyes open." "But quiet – eh?" he urged, anxiously. "It would be awful for his reputation if anybody here—" I promised a complete discretion with great gravity. "I have a canoe and three black fellows waiting not very far. I am off. Could you give me a few Martini-Henry cartridges?" I could, and did, with proper secrecy. He helped himself, with a wink at me, to a handful of my tobacco. "Between sailors – you know – good English tobacco." At the door of the pilot-house he turned round – "I say, haven't you a pair of shoes you could spare?" He raised one leg. "Look." The soles were tied with knotted strings sandal-wise under his bare feet. I rooted out an old pair, at which he looked with admiration before tucking it under his left arm. One of his pockets (bright red) was bulging with cartridges, from the other (dark blue) peeped "Towson's Inquiry," &c., &c. He seemed to think himself excellently well equipped for a re-newed encounter with the wilderness. "Ah! I'll never, never meet such a man again. You ought to have heard him recite poetry – his own too it was, he told me. Poetry!" He rolled his eyes at the recollection of these delights. "Oh, he enlarged my mind!" "Good-bye," said I. He shook hands and vanished in the night. Sometimes I ask myself whether I had ever really seen him – whether it was possible to meet such a phenomenon! . . .

'When I woke up shortly after midnight his warning came to my mind with its hint of danger that seemed, in the starred darkness, real enough to make me get up for the purpose of having a look round. On the hill a big fire burned, illuminating fitfully a crooked corner of the station-house. One of the agents with a picket of a few of our blacks, armed for the purpose, was keeping guard over the ivory; but deep within the forest, red gleams that wavered, that seemed to sink and rise from the ground amongst confused columnar shapes of intense blackness, showed the exact position of the camp where Mr Kurtz's adorers were keeping their uneasy vigil.

The monotonous beating of a big drum filled the air with muffled shocks and a lingering vibration. A steady droning sound of many men chanting each to himself some weird incantation came out from the black, flat wall of the woods as the humming of bees comes out of a hive, and had a strange narcotic effect upon my half-awake senses. I believe I dozed off leaning over the rail, till an abrupt burst of yells, an overwhelming outbreak of a pent-up and mysterious frenzy, woke me up in a bewildered wonder. It was cut short all at once, and the low droning went on with an effect of audible and soothing silence. I glanced casually into the little cabin. A light was burning within, but Mr Kurtz was not there.

'I think I would have raised an outcry if I had believed my eyes. But I didn't believe them at first – the thing seemed so impossible. The fact is, I was completely unnerved by a sheer blank fright, pure abstract terror, unconnected with any distinct shape of physical danger. What made this emotion so overpowering was – how shall I define it? – the moral shock I received, as if something altogether monstrous, intolerable to thought and odious to the soul, had been thrust upon me unexpectedly. This lasted of course the merest fraction of a second, and then the usual sense of commonplace, deadly danger, the possibility of a sudden onslaught and massacre, or something of the kind, which I saw impending, was positively welcome and composing. It pacified me, in fact, so much, that I did not raise an alarm.

'There was an agent buttoned up inside an ulster and sleeping on a chair on deck within three feet of me. The yells had not awakened him; he snored very slightly; I left him to his slumbers and leaped ashore. I did not betray Mr Kurtz – it was ordered I should never betray him – it was written I should be loyal to the nightmare of my choice. I was anxious to deal with this shadow by myself alone, – and to this day I don't know why I was so jealous of sharing with any one the peculiar blackness of that experience.

'As soon as I got on the bank I saw a trail – a broad trail through the grass. I remember the exultation with which I said to myself, "He can't walk – he is crawling on all-fours – I've got him." The grass was wet with dew. I strode rapidly with clenched fists. I fancy I had some vague notion of falling upon him and giving him a drubbing. I don't know. I had some imbecile thoughts. The knitting old woman with the cat obtruded herself upon my memory as a most improper person to be sitting at the other end of such an affair. I saw a row of pilgrims squirting lead in the air out of Winchesters held to the hip. I thought I would never get back to the steamer, and imagined myself living alone and unarmed in the woods to an advanced age. Such silly things – you know. And I remember I confounded the beat of the drum with the beating of my heart, and was pleased at its calm regularity.

'I kept to the track though – then stopped to listen. The night was very clear: a dark blue space, sparkling with dew and starlight, in which black things stood very still. I thought I could see a kind of motion ahead of me. I was strangely cocksure of everything that night. I actually left the track and ran in a wide semicircle (I verily believe chuckling to myself) so as to get in front of that stir, of that motion I had seen – if indeed I had seen anything. I was circumventing Kurtz as though it had been a boyish game.

'I came upon him, and, if he had not heard me coming, I would have fallen over him too, but he got up in time. He rose, unsteady, long, pale, indistinct, like a vapour exhaled by the earth, and swayed slightly, misty and silent before me; while at my back the fires loomed between the trees, and the murmur of many voices issued from the forest. I had cut him off cleverly; but when actually confronting him I seemed to come to my senses, I saw the danger in its right proportion. It was by no means over yet. Suppose he began to shout? Though he could hardly stand, there was still plenty of vigour in his voice. "Go away – hide yourself," he said, in that profound tone. It was very awful. I glanced back. We were within thirty yards from the nearest fire. A black figure[108] stood up, strode on long black legs, waving long black arms, across the glow. It had horns – antelope horns, I think – on its head. Some sorcerer, some witch-man, no doubt: it looked fiend-like enough. "Do you know what you are doing?" I whispered. "Perfectly," he answered, raising his voice for that single word: it sounded to me far off and yet loud, like a hail through a speaking-trumpet. If he makes a row we are lost, I thought to myself. This clearly was not a case for fisticuffs, even apart from the very natural aversion I had to beat that Shadow – this wandering and tormented thing. "You will be lost," I said – "utterly lost." One gets sometimes such a flash of inspiration, you know. I did say the right thing, though indeed he could not have been more irretrievably lost than he was at this very moment, when the foundations of our intimacy were being laid – to endure – to endure – even to the end – even beyond.

'"I had immense plans," he muttered irresolutely. "Yes," said I; "but if you try to shout I'll smash your head with—" there was not a stick or a stone near. "I will throttle you for good," I corrected myself. "I was on the threshold of great things," he pleaded, in a voice of longing, with a wistfulness of tone that made my blood run cold. "And now for this stupid scoundrel—" "Your success in Europe is assured in any case," I affirmed, steadily. I did not want to have the throttling of him, you understand – and indeed it would have been very little use for any practical purpose. I tried to break the spell – the heavy, mute spell of the wilderness – that seemed to draw him to its pitiless breast by the awakening of forgotten and brutal instincts, by the memory of gratified and monstrous passions. This alone, I was convinced, had driven him out to the edge of the forest, to the bush, towards the gleam of fires, the throb of drums, the drone of weird incantations; this alone had beguiled his unlawful soul beyond the bounds of permitted aspirations. And, don't you see, the terror of the position was not in being knocked on the head – though I had a very lively sense of that danger too – but in this, that I had to deal with a being to whom I could not appeal in the name of anything high or low. I had, even like the niggers, to invoke him – himself – his own exalted and incredible degradation. There was nothing either above or below him, and I knew it. He had kicked himself loose of the earth. Confound the man! he had kicked the very earth to pieces. He was alone, and I before him did not know whether I stood on the ground or floated in the air. I've been telling you what we said – repeating the phrases we pronounced, – but what's the good? They were common everyday words, – the familiar, vague sounds exchanged on every waking day of life. But what of that? They had behind them, to my mind, the terrific suggestiveness of words heard in dreams, of phrases spoken in nightmares. Soul! If anybody had ever struggled with a soul,[109] I am the man. And I wasn't arguing with a lunatic either. Believe me or not, his intelligence was perfectly clear – concentrated, it is true, upon himself with horrible intensity, yet clear; and therein was my only chance – barring, of course, the killing him there and then, which wasn't so good, on account of unavoidable noise. But his soul was mad. Being alone in the wilderness, it had looked within itself, and, by heavens! I tell you, it had gone mad. I had – for my sins, I suppose – to go through the ordeal of looking into it myself. No eloquence could have been so withering to one's belief in mankind as his final burst of sincerity. He struggled with himself, too. I saw it, – I heard it. I saw the inconceivable mystery of a soul that knew no restraint, no faith, and no fear, yet struggling blindly with itself. I kept my head pretty well; but when I had him at last stretched on the couch, I wiped my forehead, while my legs shook under me as though I had carried half a ton on my back down that hill. And yet I had only supported him, his bony arm clasped round my neck – and he was not much heavier than a child.

'When next day we left at noon, the crowd, of whose presence behind the curtain of trees I had been acutely conscious all the time, flowed out of the woods again, filled the clearing, covered the slope with a mass of naked, breathing, quivering, bronze bodies. I steamed up a bit, then swung down-stream, and two thousand eyes followed the evolutions of the splashing, thumping, fierce river-demon[110] beating the water with its terrible tail and breathing black smoke into the air. In front of the first rank, along the river, three men, plastered with bright red earth from head to foot, strutted to and fro restlessly. When we came abreast again, they faced the river, stamped their feet, nodded their horned heads, swayed their scarlet bodies; they shook towards the fierce river-demon a bunch of black feathers, a mangy skin with a pendent tail – something that looked like a dried gourd; they shouted periodically together strings of amazing words that resembled no sounds of human language; and the deep murmurs of the crowd, interrupted suddenly, were like the responses of some satanic litany.

'We had carried Kurtz into the pilot-house: there was more air there. Lying on the couch, he stared through the open shutter. There was an eddy in the mass of human bodies, and the woman with helmeted head and tawny cheeks rushed out to the very brink of the stream. She put out her hands, shouted something, and all that wild mob took up the shout in a roaring chorus of articulated, rapid, breathless utterance.

'"Do you understand this?" I asked.

'He kept on looking out past me with fiery, longing eyes, with a mingled expression of wistfulness and hate. He made no answer, but I saw a smile, a smile of indefinable meaning, appear on his colourless lips that a moment after twitched convulsively. "Do I not?" he said slowly, gasping, as if the words had been torn out of him by a supernatural power.

'I pulled the string of the whistle, and I did this because I saw the pilgrims on deck getting out their rifles with an air of anticipating a jolly lark. At the sudden screech there was a movement of abject terror through that wedged mass of bodies. "Don't! don't! you frighten them away," cried some one on deck disconsolately. I pulled the string time after time. They broke and ran, they leaped, they crouched, they swerved, they dodged the flying terror of the sound. The three red chaps had fallen flat, face down on the shore, as though they had been shot dead. Only the barbarous and superb woman did not so much as flinch, and stretched tragically her bare arms after us over the sombre and glittering river.

'And then that imbecile crowd down on the deck started their little fun, and I could see nothing more for smoke.

'The brown current ran swiftly out of the heart of darkness, bearing us down towards the sea with twice the speed of our upward progress; and Kurtz's life was running swiftly too, ebbing, ebbing out of his heart into the sea of inexorable time. The manager was very placid, he had no vital anxieties now, he took us both in with a comprehensive and satisfied glance: the "affair" had come off as well as could be wished. I saw the time approaching when I would be left alone of the party of "unsound method." The pilgrims looked upon me with disfavour. I was, so to speak, numbered with the dead. It is strange how I accepted this unforeseen partnership, this choice of nightmares forced upon me in the tenebrous land invaded by these mean and greedy phantoms.

'Kurtz discoursed. A voice! a voice! It rang deep to the very last. It survived his strength to hide in the magnificent folds of eloquence the barren darkness of his heart. Oh, he struggled! he struggled! The wastes of his weary brain were haunted by shadowy images now – images of wealth and fame revolving obsequiously round his unextinguishable gift of noble and lofty expression. My Intended, my station, my career, my ideas – these were the subjects for the occasional utterances of elevated sentiments. The shade of the original Kurtz frequented the bedside of the hollow sham, whose fate it was to be buried presently in the mould of primeval earth. But both the diabolic love and the unearthly hate of the mysteries it had penetrated fought for the possession of that soul satiated with primitive emotions, avid of lying fame, of sham distinction, of all the appearances of success and power.

'Sometimes he was contemptibly childish. He desired to have kings meet him at railway-stations[111] on his return from some ghastly Nowhere, where he intended to accomplish great things. "You show them you have in you something that is really profitable, and then there will be no limits to the recognition of your ability," he would say. "Of course you must take care of the motives – right motives – always." The long reaches that were like one and the same reach, monotonous bends that were exactly alike, slipped past the steamer with their multitude of secular trees looking patiently after this grimy fragment of another world, the forerunner of change, of conquest, of trade, of massacres, of blessings. I looked ahead – piloting. "Close the shutter," said Kurtz suddenly one day; "I can't bear to look at this." I did so. There was a silence. "Oh, but I will wring your heart yet!" he cried at the invisible wilderness.

'We broke down – as I had expected – and had to lie up for repairs at the head of an island. This delay was the first thing that shook Kurtz's confidence. One morning he gave me a packet of papers and a photograph, – the lot tied together with a shoe-string. "Keep this for me," he said. "This noxious fool" (meaning the manager) "is capable of prying into my boxes when I am not looking." In the afternoon I saw him. He was lying on his back with closed eyes, and I withdrew quietly, but I heard him mutter, "Live rightly, die, die . . ." I listened. There was nothing more. Was he rehearsing some speech in his sleep, or was it a fragment of a phrase from some newspaper article? He had been writing for the papers and meant to do so again, "for the furthering of my ideas. It's a duty."

'His was an impenetrable darkness. I looked at him as you peer down at a man who is lying at the bottom of a precipice where the sun never shines. But I had not much time to give him, because I was helping the engine-driver to take to pieces the leaky cylinders, to straighten a bent connecting-rod, and in other such matters. I lived in an infernal mess of rust, filings, nuts, bolts, spanners, hammers, ratchet-drills – things I abominate, because I don't get on with them. I tended the little forge we fortunately had aboard; I toiled wearily in a wretched scrap-heap – unless I had the shakes too bad to stand.

'One evening coming in with a candle I was startled to hear him say a little tremulously, "I am lying here in the dark waiting for death." The light was within a foot of his eyes. I forced myself to murmur, "Oh, nonsense!" and stood over him as if transfixed.

'Anything approaching the change that came over his features I have never seen before, and hope never to see again. Oh, I wasn't touched. I was fascinated. It was as though a veil had been rent. I saw on that ivory face the expression of sombre pride, of ruthless power, of craven terror – of an intense and hopeless despair. Did he live his life again in every detail of desire, temptation, and surrender during that supreme moment of complete knowledge? He cried in a whisper at some image, at some vision, – he cried out twice, a cry that was no more than a breath –

'"The horror! The horror!"[112]

'I blew the candle out and left the cabin. The pilgrims were dining in the mess-room, and I took my place opposite the manager, who lifted his eyes to give me a questioning glance, which I successfully ignored. He leaned back, serene, with that peculiar smile of his sealing the unexpressed depths of his meanness. A continuous shower of small flies streamed upon the lamp, upon the cloth, upon our hands and faces. Suddenly the manager's boy put his insolent black head in the doorway, and said in a tone of scathing contempt –

'"Mistah Kurtz – he dead."

'All the pilgrims rushed out to see. I remained, and went on with my dinner. I believe I was considered brutally callous. However, I did not eat much. There was a lamp in there – light, don't you know – and outside it was so beastly, beastly dark. I went no more near the remarkable man who had pronounced a judgment upon the adventures of his soul on this earth. The voice was gone. What else had been there? But I am of course aware that next day the pilgrims buried something in a muddy hole.

'And then they very nearly buried me.

'However, as you see, I did not go to join Kurtz there and then. I did not. I remained to dream the nightmare out to the end, and to show my loyalty to Kurtz once more. Destiny. My destiny! Droll thing life is – that mysterious arrangement of merciless logic for a futile purpose. The most you can hope from it is some knowledge of yourself – that comes too late – a crop of unextinguishable regrets. I have wrestled with death. It is the most unexciting contest you can imagine. It takes place in an impalpable greyness, with nothing underfoot, with nothing around, without spectators, without clamour, without glory, without the great desire of victory, without the great fear of defeat, in a sickly atmosphere of tepid scepticism, without much belief in your own right, and still less in that of your adversary. If such is the form of ultimate wisdom, then life is a greater riddle than some of us think it to be. I was within a hair's-breadth of the last opportunity for pronounce-ment, and I found with humiliation that probably I would have nothing to say. This is the reason why I affirm that Kurtz was a remarkable man. He had something to say. He said it. Since I had peeped over the edge[113] myself, I under-stand better the meaning of his stare, that could not see the flame of the candle, but was wide enough to embrace the whole universe, piercing enough to penetrate all the hearts that beat in the darkness. He had summed up – he had judged. "The horror!" He was a remarkable man. After all, this was the expression of some sort of belief; it had candour, it had conviction, it had a vibrating note of revolt in its whisper, it had the appalling face of a glimpsed truth – the strange commingling of desire and hate. And it is not my own extremity I remember best – a vision of greyness without form filled with physical pain, and a careless contempt for the evanescence of all things – even of this pain itself. No! It is his extremity that I seem to have lived through. True, he had made that last stride, he had stepped over the edge, while I had been permitted to draw back my hesitating foot. And perhaps in this is the whole difference; perhaps all the wisdom, and all truth, and all sincerity, are just compressed into that inappreciable moment of time in which we step over the threshold of the invisible. Perhaps! I like to think my summing-up would not have been a word of careless contempt. Better his cry – much better. It was an affirmation, a moral victory paid for by innumerable defeats, by abominable terrors, by abominable satisfactions. But it was a victory! That is why I have remained loyal to Kurtz to the last, and even beyond, when a long time after I heard once more, not his own voice, but the echo of his magnificent eloquence thrown to me from a soul as translucently pure as a cliff of crystal.

'No, they did not bury me, though there is a period of time which I remember mistily, with a shuddering wonder, like a passage through some inconceivable world that had no hope in it and no desire. I found myself back in the sepulchral city resenting the sight of people hurrying through the streets to filch a little money from each other, to devour their infamous cookery, to gulp their unwholesome beer, to dream their insignificant and silly dreams. They trespassed upon my thoughts. They were intruders whose knowledge of life was to me an irritating pretence, because I felt so sure they could not possibly know the things I knew. Their bearing, which was simply the bearing of commonplace individuals going about their business in the assurance of perfect safety, was offensive to me like the outrageous flauntings of folly in the face of a danger it is unable to comprehend.[114] I had no particular desire to enlighten them, but I had some difficulty in restraining myself from laughing in their faces, so full of stupid importance. I daresay I was not very well at that time. I tottered about the streets – there were various affairs to settle – grinning bitterly at perfectly respectable persons. I admit my behaviour was inexcusable, but then my temperature was seldom normal in these days. My dear aunt's endeavours to "nurse up my strength" seemed altogether beside the mark. It was not my strength that wanted nursing, it was my imagina-

tion that wanted soothing. I kept the bundle of papers given
me by Kurtz, not knowing exactly what to do with it. His
mother had died lately, watched over, as I was told, by his
Intended. A clean-shaved man, with an official manner and
wearing gold-rimmed spectacles, called on me one day and
made inquiries, at first circuitous, afterwards suavely pressing,
about what he was pleased to denominate certain "documents."
I was not surprised, because I had had two rows with the
manager on the subject out there. I had refused to give up the
smallest scrap out of that package, and I took the same
attitude with the spectacled man. He became darkly menacing
at last, and with much heat argued that the Company had the
right to every bit of information about its "territories." And,
said he, "Mr Kurtz's knowledge of unexplored regions must
have been necessarily extensive and peculiar – owing to his
great abilities and to the deplorable circumstances in which he
had been placed: therefore—" I assured him Mr Kurtz's
knowledge, however extensive, did not bear upon the problems
of commerce or administration. He invoked then the name of
science. "It would be an incalculable loss if," &c., &c. I
offered him the report on the "Suppression of Savage Customs," with the postscriptum torn off. He took it up eagerly,
but ended by sniffing at it with an air of contempt. "This is
not what we had a right to expect," he remarked. "Expect
nothing else," I said. "There are only private letters." He
withdrew upon some threat of legal proceedings, and I saw
him no more; but another fellow, calling himself Kurtz's
cousin, appeared two days later, and was anxious to hear all
the details about his dear relative's last moments. Incidentally
he gave me to understand that Kurtz had been essentially a
great musician. "There was the making of an immense success," said the man, who was an organist, I believe, with lank
grey hair flowing over a greasy coat-collar. I had no reason to

doubt his statement; and to this day I am unable to say what
was Kurtz's profession, whether he ever had any – which was
the greatest of his talents. I had taken him for a painter who
wrote for the papers, or else for a journalist who could paint –
but even the cousin (who took snuff during the interview)
could not tell me what he had been – exactly. He was a
univers. ! genius – on that point I agreed with the old chap,
who thereupon blew his nose noisily into a large cotton
handkerchief and withdrew in senile agitation, bearing off
some family letters and memoranda without importance. Ultimately a journalist anxious to know something of the fate of
his "dear colleague" turned up. This visitor informed me
Kurtz's proper sphere ought to have been politics "on the
popular side." He had furry straight eyebrows, bristly hair
cropped short, an eye-glass on a broad ribbon, and, becoming
expansive, confessed his opinion that Kurtz really couldn't
write a bit – "but heavens! how that man could talk! He
electrified large meetings. He had faith – don't you see? – he
had the faith. He could get himself to believe anything –
anything. He would have been a splendid leader of an extreme
party." "What party?" I asked. "Any party," answered the
other. "He was an – an – extremist." Did I not think so? I
assented. Did I know, he asked, with a sudden flash of
curiosity, "what it was that had induced him to go out there?"
"Yes," said I, and forthwith handed him the famous Report
for publication, if he thought fit. He glanced through it
hurriedly, mumbling all the time, judged "it would do," and
took himself off with this plunder.

'Thus I was left at last with a slim packet of letters and the
girl's portrait. She struck me as beautiful – I mean she had a
beautiful expression. I know that the sunlight can be made to
lie too, yet one felt that no manipulation of light and pose
could have conveyed the delicate shade of truthfulness upon

those features. She seemed ready to listen without mental reservation, without suspicion, without a thought for herself. I concluded I would go and give her back her portrait and those letters myself. Curiosity? Yes; and also some other feeling perhaps.[115] All that had been Kurtz's had passed out of my hands: his soul, his body, his station, his plans, his ivory, his career. There remained only his memory and his Intended – and I wanted to give that up too to the past, in a way, – to surrender personally all that remained of him with me to that oblivion which is the last word of our common fate. I don't defend myself. I had no clear perception of what it was I really wanted. Perhaps it was an impulse of unconscious loyalty, or the fulfilment of one of those ironic necessities that lurk in the facts of human existence. I don't know. I can't tell. But I went.

'I thought his memory was like the other memories of the dead that accumulate in every man's life, – a vague impress on the brain of shadows that had fallen on it in their swift and final passage; but before the high and ponderous door, between the tall houses of a street as still and decorous as a well-kept alley in a cemetery, I had a vision of him on the stretcher, opening his mouth voraciously, as if to devour all the earth with all its mankind. He lived then before me; he lived as much as he had ever lived – a shadow insatiable of splendid appearances, of frightful realities; a shadow darker than the shadow of the night, and draped nobly in the folds of a gorgeous eloquence. The vision seemed to enter the house with me – the stretcher, the phantom-bearers, the wild crowd of obedient worshippers, the gloom of the forests, the glitter of the reach between the murky bends, the beat of the drum, regular and muffled like the beating of a heart – the heart of a conquering darkness. It was a moment of triumph for the wilderness, an invading and vengeful rush which, it seemed to me, I would have to keep back alone for the salvation of another soul. And the memory of what I had heard him say afar there, with the horned shapes stirring at my back, in the glow of fires, within the patient woods, those broken phrases came back to me, were heard again in their ominous and terrifying simplicity. I remembered his abject pleading, his abject threats, the colossal scale of his vile desires, the meanness, the torment, the tempestuous anguish of his soul. And later on I seemed to see his collected languid manner, when he said one day, "This lot of ivory now is really mine. The Company did not pay for it. I collected it myself at a very great personal risk. I am afraid they will try to claim it as theirs though. H'm. It is a difficult case. What do you think I ought to do – resist? Eh? I want no more than justice." . . . He wanted no more than justice – no more than justice. I rang the bell before a mahogany door on the first floor, and while I waited he seemed to stare at me out of the glassy panel[116] – stare with that wide and immense stare embracing, condemning, loathing all the universe. I seemed to hear the whispered cry, "The horror! The horror!"

'The dusk was falling. I had to wait in a lofty drawing-room with three long windows from floor to ceiling that were like three luminous and bedraped columns. The bent gilt legs and backs of the furniture shone in indistinct curves. The tall marble fireplace had a cold and monumental whiteness. A grand piano stood massively in a corner, with dark gleams on the flat surfaces like a sombre and polished sarcophagus. A high door opened – closed. I rose.

'She came forward, all in black, with a pale head, floating towards me in the dusk. She was in mourning. It was more than a year since his death, more than a year since the news came; she seemed as though she would remember and mourn for ever. She took both my hands in hers and murmured, "I had heard you were coming." I noticed she was not very young – I mean not girlish. She had a mature capacity for fidelity, for belief, for suffering. The room seemed to have grown darker, as if all the sad light of the cloudy evening had taken refuge on her forehead. This fair hair, this pale visage, this pure brow, seemed surrounded by an ashy halo from which the dark eyes looked out at me. Their glance was guileless, profound, confident, and trustful. She carried her sorrowful head as though she were proud of that sorrow, as though she would say, I – I alone know how to mourn for him as he deserves. But while we were still shaking hands, such a look of awful desolation came upon her face that I perceived she was one of those creatures that are not the playthings of Time. For her he had died only yesterday. And, by Jove! the impression was so powerful that for me too he seemed to have died only yesterday – nay, this very minute. I saw her and him in the same instant of time – his death and her sorrow – I saw her sorrow in the very moment of his death. Do you understand? I saw them together – I heard them together. She had said, with a deep catch of the breath, "I have survived"; while my strained ears seemed to hear distinctly, mingled with her tone of despairing regret, the summing-up whisper of his eternal condemnation. I asked myself what I was doing there, with a sensation of panic in my heart as though I had blundered into a place of cruel and absurd mysteries not fit for a human being to behold. She motioned me to a chair. We sat down. I laid the packet gently on the little table, and she put her hand over it. ... "You knew him well," she murmured, after a moment of mourning silence.

'"Intimacy grows quickly out there," I said. "I knew him as well as it is possible for one man to know another."

'"And you admired him," she said. "It was impossible to know him and not to admire him. Was it?"

'"He was a remarkable man," I said, unsteadily. Then before the appealing fixity of her gaze, that seemed to watch for more words on my lips, I went on, "It was impossible not to—"

'"Love him," she finished eagerly, silencing me into an appalled dumbness. "How true! how true! But when you think that no one knew him so well as I! I had all his noble confidence. I knew him best."

'"You knew him best," I repeated. And perhaps she did. But with every word spoken the room was growing darker, and only her forehead, smooth and white, remained illumined by the unextinguishable light of belief and love.

'"You were his friend," she went on. "His friend," she repeated, a little louder. "You must have been, if he had given you this, and sent you to me. I feel I can speak to you – and oh! I must speak. I want you – you who have heard his last words – to know I have been worthy of him. . . . It is not pride. . . . Yes! I am proud to know I understood him better than any one on earth – he told me so himself. And since his mother died I have had no one – no one – to – to—"

'I listened. The darkness deepened. I was not even sure whether he had given me the right bundle. I rather suspect he wanted me to take care of another batch of his papers which, after his death, I saw the manager examining under the lamp. And the girl talked, easing her pain in the certitude of my sympathy; she talked as thirsty men drink. I had heard that her engagement with Kurtz had been disapproved by her people. He wasn't rich enough or something. And indeed I don't know whether he had not been a pauper all his life. He had given me some reason to infer that it was his impatience of comparative poverty that drove him out there.

'". . . Who was not his friend who had heard him speak

once?" she was saying. "He drew men towards him by what was best in them." She looked at me with intensity. "It is the gift of the great," she went on, and the sound of her low voice seemed to have the accompaniment of all the other sounds, full of mystery, desolation, and sorrow, I had ever heard – the ripple of the river, the soughing of the trees swayed by the wind, the murmurs of wild crowds, the faint ring of incomprehensible words cried from afar, the whisper of a voice speaking from beyond the threshold of an eternal darkness. "But you have heard him! You know!" she cried.

'"Yes, I know," I said with something like despair in my heart, but bowing my head before the faith that was in her, before that great and saving illusion that shone with an unearthly glow in the darkness, in the triumphant darkness from which I could not have defended her – from which I could not even defend myself.

'"What a loss to me – to us!" – she corrected herself with beautiful generosity; then added in a murmur, "To the world." By the last gleams of twilight I could see the glitter of her eyes, full of tears – of tears that would not fall.

'"I have been very happy – very fortunate – very proud," she went on. "Too fortunate. Too happy for a little while. And now I am unhappy for – for life."

'She stood up; her fair hair seemed to catch all the remaining light in a glimmer of gold. I rose too.

'"And of all this," she went on, mournfully, "of all his promise, and of all his greatness, of his generous mind, of his noble heart, nothing remains – nothing but a memory. You and I—"

'"We shall always remember him," I said, hastily.

'"No!" she cried. "It is impossible that all this should be lost – that such a life should be sacrificed to leave nothing – but sorrow. You know what vast plans he had. I knew of them too – I could not perhaps understand, – but others knew of them. Something must remain. His words, at least, have not died."

'"His words will remain," I said.

'"And his example," she whispered to herself. "Men looked up to him, – his goodness shone in every act. His example—"

'"True," I said; "his example too. Yes, his example. I forgot that."

'"But I do not. I cannot – I cannot believe – not yet. I cannot believe that I shall never see him again, that nobody will see him again, never, never, never."

'She put out her arms as if after a retreating figure, stretching them black and with clasped pale hands across the fading and narrow sheen of the window. Never see him! I saw him clearly enough then. I shall see this eloquent phantom as long as I live, and I shall see her too, a tragic and familiar Shade, resembling in this gesture another one, tragic also, and bedecked with powerless charms, stretching bare brown arms over the glitter of the infernal stream, the stream of darkness. She said suddenly very low, "He died as he lived."

'"His end," said I, with dull anger stirring in me, "was in every way worthy of his life."

'"And I was not with him," she murmured. My anger subsided before a feeling of infinite pity.

'"Everything that could be done—" I mumbled.

'"Ah, but I believed in him more than any one on earth – more than his own mother, more than – himself. He needed me! Me! I would have treasured every sigh, every word, every sign, every glance."

'I felt like a chill grip on my chest. "Don't," I said, in a muffled voice.

' "Forgive me. I – I – have mourned so long in silence – in silence. . . . You were with him – to the last? I think of his loneliness. Nobody near to understand him as I would have understood. Perhaps no one to hear . . ."

' "To the very end," I said, shakily. "I heard his very last words. . . ." I stopped in a fright.

' "Repeat them," she said in a heart-broken tone. "I want – I want – something – something – to – to live with."

'I was on the point of crying at her, "Don't you hear them?" The dusk was repeating them in a persistent whisper all around us, in a whisper that seemed to swell menacingly like the first whisper of a rising wind. "The horror! the horror!"

' "His last word – to live with," she murmured. "Don't you understand I loved him – I loved him – I loved him!"

'I pulled myself together and spoke slowly.

' "The last word he pronounced was – your name."

'I heard a light sigh, and then my heart stood still, stopped dead short by an exulting and terrible cry, by the cry of inconceivable triumph and of unspeakable pain. "I knew it – I was sure!" . . . She knew. She was sure. I heard her weeping; she had hidden her face in her hands. It seemed to me that the house would collapse before I could escape, that the heavens would fall upon my head. But nothing happened. The heavens do not fall[117] for such a trifle. Would they have fallen, I wonder, if I had rendered Kurtz that justice which was his due? Hadn't he said he wanted only justice? But I couldn't. I could not tell her. It would have been too dark – too dark altogether. . . .'

Marlow ceased, and sat apart, indistinct and silent, in the pose of a meditating Buddha. Nobody moved for a time. 'We have lost the first of the ebb,' said the Director, suddenly. I raised my head. The offing was barred by a black bank of clouds, and the tranquil waterway leading to the uttermost ends of the earth flowed sombre under an overcast sky – seemed to lead into the heart of an immense darkness.

NOTES ON *HEART OF DARKNESS*

Author's Note

1. *this volume*: *Youth: A Narrative; and Two Other Stories* (Edinburgh & London: William Blackwood & Sons, 1902).

2. Maga: Familiar abbreviation for *Blackwood's Edinburgh Magazine*.

3. *first contribution*: This was 'Karain' in November 1897.

4. *Marlow*: Marlow was to appear again as narrator in *Lord Jim* and *Chance*. Marlow is the most important of Conrad's transtextual characters. For an account of Conrad's transtextual narratives, see Cedric Watts, *The Deceptive Text: An Introduction to Covert Plots* (Brighton: Harvester Press, 1984), pp. 133–50.

5. *be gone*: Compare *Othello*, III.iii.357.

6. *Solomonian sense*: See Ecclesiastes 1:14.

7. *my first command*: The *Otago*, an Australian-owned barque. Conrad took over the command after the death of the captain. He had signed off the *Vidar* on 4 January 1888 and lodged at the Sailors' Home in Singapore. He received notice of the command on 19 January and joined the ship in Bangkok on 24 January. The first stage of the voyage, beset by calms in the Gulf of Siam and illness among the crew, provides the basis for the story 'The Shadow-Line'; a later voyage, from Mauritius to Sydney, lies behind the story 'A Smile of Fortune'. Conrad resigned his command in March 1889.

8. *one other*: That is, 'An Outpost of Progress'.

Heart of Darkness

1. *The* Nellie: During the summer of 1891 Conrad visited his friend G.F.W. Hope in Stanford, Essex, and made two trips in Hope's yawl, the *Nellie*, along the Thames estuary. See Owen Knowles, *A Conrad Chronology* (Basingstoke: Macmillan, 1989), p. 16.

2. *Gravesend*: Town twenty-six miles east of London, on the Kent shore of the Thames estuary.

3. *town on earth*: For a discussion of the representation of London in Conrad's fiction, see the essays by Cedric Watts, Juliet McLauchlan, Robert Hampson, Hugh Epstein and Martin Ray in Gene M. Moore (ed.), *Conrad's Cities: Essays for Hans van Marle* (Amsterdam/Atlanta, Georgia: Rodopi, 1992).

4. *We four*: The group of men described here had appeared already in 'Youth' (*Blackwood's Edinburgh Magazine*, September 1898) as the audience for one of Marlow's tales. They were based on a group of Conrad's friends: G.F.W. Hope (a company director); W.B. Keen (an accountant); and T.L. Mears (a lawyer).

5. *a pilot*: The typescript contains a fuller description: 'The sunburnt neck, the broad shoulders, the set of the blue clothes, the balance and solid aspect of the whole figure suggested the idealized type of a pilot . . .'

6. *somewhere*: This refers to the second paragraph of 'Youth': 'We all began life in the merchant service. Between the five of us there was the strong bond of the sea, and also the fellowship of the craft . . .'

7. *the bones*: That is, dominoes, which, at this time, were often made of ivory. In his memoir Hope mentions that he, Conrad, Keen and Mears used to play dominoes on board the *Nellie*.

8. *an idol*: Note Conrad's later comparisons of Marlow to 'a Buddha preaching' (p. 20) and 'a meditating Buddha' (p. 123). These comparisons are partly ironic and partly straight. On the one hand, if Marlow is the possessor of knowledge, it is the knowledge of a 'heart of darkness' rather than of enlightenment. On the other hand, Marlow as story-teller can be seen as offering a teaching-tale comparable to the Buddhist *Jataka*. For some of the critical discussion of this point, see William Bysshe Stein, 'Buddhism and the *Heart of Darkness*', *Western Humanities Review*, 11 (1957), pp. 281–5; W.B. Stein, 'The Lotus Posture and *Heart of Darkness*', *Modern Fiction Studies*, 2 (Winter 1956/7), pp. 235–7; H.C.

Brashers, 'Conrad, Marlow and Gautama Buddha', *Conradiana*, 1 (1969), pp. 63–71; W.B. Stein, 'The Heart of Darkness: A Bodhisattva Scenario', *Conradiana*, 2 (1969–70), pp. 39–52; William W. Bonney, *Thorns & Arabesques* (Baltimore/London: Johns Hopkins, 1980); Peter Caracciolo, 'Buddhist Teaching Stories and Their Influence on Conrad, Wells, and Kipling', the *Conradian*, 11.1 (May 1986), pp. 24–34; Peter Caracciolo, 'Buddhist Typologies in *Heart of Darkness* and *Victory*', the *Conradian*, 14.1/2 (December 1989), pp. 67–91.

9. *Sir Francis Drake*: Sir Francis Drake (1545–96) is cited here because of the expedition that made him famous. In 1577 he proposed a voyage into the South Seas through the Straits of Magellan, a voyage that no Englishman had so far attempted. When he returned in 1580, he was the first man to have circumnavigated the globe.

10. *Sir John Franklin*: Sir John Franklin (1786–1847) began his career exploring and mapping the coast of Australia. From 1819 onwards he was involved in various attempts to find the North-West Passage to the Pacific. In 1845 he sailed from Greenhithe on what turned out to be a successful quest for the North-West Passage but also his last expedition. See F.L. McClintock, *The Voyage of the 'Fox' in the Arctic Seas* (London: John Murray, 1859) and 'Introduction', pp. xiv–xvi.

11. *the* Golden Hind: The ship in which Sir Francis Drake circum-navigated the globe. Soon after the ship arrived in Deptford, Queen Elizabeth I went on board to confer a knighthood on Drake.

12. *the* Erebus *and* Terror: The two ships that made up Sir John Franklin's 1845 expedition. The ships became icebound, and the men all died from a combination of cold, disease and starvation. Dr Rae (1854) was the first to find evidence that some of them had resorted to cannibalism in an attempt to save their lives. The most recent study of the expedition is David C. Woodman, *Unravelling the Franklin Mystery: Inuit Testimony* (Montreal: McGill-Queen's University Press, 1992).

13. *on 'Change*: The place where merchants met for the transaction of business.

14. *'interlopers'*: Ships engaged in unauthorized trading, i.e., ships that, without belonging to companies chartered by the Crown and without having a licence from such companies, traded with the countries to which these companies asserted sole trade – here, specifically, in breach of the East India Company monopoly.

15. *commissioned 'generals'*: That is, general merchants, dealers in many kinds of goods.

16. *the dark places of the earth*: Compare William Booth, in *In Darkest England* (London: Salvation Army [1890]): 'As there is a darkest Africa is there not also a darkest England?' (p. 11). Booth was responding, in part, to the publication of Henry M. Stanley's book, *In Darkest Africa* (London, 1890), his account of the expedition he led to rescue Emin Pasha, the Governor of the Equatorial Provinces, from the Mahdi's troops. For a discussion of this trope, see Robert Hampson, 'Conrad and the Idea of Empire', *L'Époque Conradienne* (Limoges: Société Conradienne Française, 1989), pp. 9–22.

17. *when the Romans first came here*: Again, this was a recurrent trope in imperialist discourse. Cedric Watts in his 1990 World's Classics edition of Heart of Darkness notes a speech made by Stanley (reported in *The Times*, 4 October 1892), which quoted approvingly a speech made by William Pitt in 1792:

It has been alleged that Africa labours under a natural incapacity for civilization ... Allow of this principle as applied to Africa, and I should be glad to know why it might not also have been applied to ancient and uncivilized Britain. Why might not some Roman Senator have predicted with equal boldness – 'There is a people destined never to be free, a people depressed by the hand of nature below the level of the human species, and created to form a supply of slaves for the rest of the world'? Sir, we were once as obscure among the nations of the earth, as debased in our morals, as savage in our manners, as degraded in our understandings as these unhappy Africans are at present.

There is an ironic dimension to this trope: the Romans arrived in Britain in 45 BC, and the Roman legions would have included soldiers from North Africa. The Angles and Saxons, from whom the English derive, did not arrive for several more centuries. In other words, as Peter Fryer observes in *Staying Power* (London: Pluto Press, 1984), 'There were Africans in Britain before the English came here.'

18. *you say Knights*: This is the first indication that the passage referring to Sir Francis Drake and Sir John Franklin represents a speech made by the unnamed primary narrator.

19. *what we read*: Cedric Watts offers, in his edition of *Heart of Darkness*, as an example, Caesar's *De Bello Gallico*, v, 1–2 (which suggests that 628 ships were built in one winter). In 'London's River' (1906) Conrad notes that Romans in the Thames estuary would have used a light galley and 'not a trireme'.

20. *Falernian wine*: A famous ancient wine from Campania. As William

F. Engel points out, the wine is frequently mentioned in Roman poetry, by 'nearly every poet from Catullus to Propertius, including Ovid, Virgil and Horace'. For Horace, in particular, Falernian wine symbolized 'the best that civilization has to offer'. See 'Conrad, Marlow and *Falernian*', *Conradiana*, 9.2 (1977), p. 170.

21. *Ravenna*: The chief Roman naval base in northern Italy on the upper Adriatic.

22. *to be got*: A cancelled passage in the manuscript continues 'but at any rate they had no pretty fictions about it. They had no international associations from motives of philanthropy with some third rate king for head . . .' This was replaced by an expanded version, which also appears in the typescript.

23. *green flames, red flames, white flames*: That is, ships' lights and their reflections. As Cedric Watts notes in his 1990 World's Classics edition, sailing vessels carried a green light on the starboard side and a red one on the port side; steamers carried, in addition, a white light on or in front of the foremast.

24. *the sleepless river*: In the manuscript and typescript there now follows a lengthy description of a 'big steamer' – 'a long blaze of lights like a town viewed from the sea'.

25. *a passion for maps*: In 'Geography and Some Explorers', Conrad records how his reading of McClintock's *The Voyage of the 'Fox' in the Arctic Seas* as a boy produced in him 'the taste for poring over maps' (*Last Essays* [J.M. Dent, 1926], p. 17; hereafter cited as *LE*).

26. *blank spaces*: McClintock uses this phrase a number of times in *The Voyage of the 'Fox' in the Arctic Seas* to refer to unmapped and unexplored areas of the Arctic. In 'Geography and Some Explorers', Conrad recalls the 'exciting spaces of white paper' (*LE*, p. 19) in maps of Africa and the particular excitement of entering Tanganyika 'on the blank' of his old atlas (*LE*, p. 21): 'The heart of its Africa was white and big' (*LE*, p. 20).

27. *rivers and lakes and names*: Compare 'Geography and Some Explorers'. David Livingstone, for example, had inscribed in that 'blank space' Lake Ngami in 1849, the Victoria Falls in 1855, the central Zambesi valley in 1853–6, Lake Nyasa in 1859, the river Lualaba in 1871. The 1858–9 expedition of Burton and Speke added Lake Tanganyika and Lake Victoria to the map.

28. *a Company for trade*: In November 1889 Conrad went to Brussels to be interviewed by Albert Thys of the Société Anonyme Belge pour le Commerce du Haut-Congo (the Belgian Limited Company for Trade in

the Upper Congo) with a view to captaining one of the company's river-steamers. In February 1890 he had a further interview with Thys. His appointment to the Congo was confirmed in April as a result of the efforts of his 'aunt', Marguerite Poradowska (the wife of Aleksander Poradowski, the first cousin of his maternal grandmother), and he was asked (as he understood it) to take command of the *Florida*.

29. *Fresleven*: Johannes Freiesleben, a Danish captain, Conrad's predecessor in command of the *Florida*, was killed on 29 January 1890 at Tchumberi in a dispute over hens. When his bones were recovered on 23 March 1890 by a punitive expedition under Captain Duhst, grass was growing through the skeleton, which lay where it had fallen. In *An Outcast of the Islands*, Willems imagines himself lying dead on the ground 'till there would remain nothing but the white gleam of bleaching bones in the long grass; in the long grass that would shoot its feathery heads between the bare and polished ribs' (p. 332). Hans van Marle, in his notes to the 1992 World's Classics edition, suggests that this passage might be derived from Conrad's memories of Freiesleben, although Norman Sherry suggests that Freiesleben was buried before Conrad arrived (*Conrad's Western World* [Cambridge: Cambridge University Press, 1971]; hereafter cited as Sherry). The state of Freiesleben's body is echoed in the description of the city street with 'grass sprouting between the stones' (*HD*, p. 24).

30. *stepped into his shoes*: In this context the dead metaphor has a disquieting sense of concreteness and life. Later Marlow will be eager to discard a pair of his own shoes (*HD* p. 79), and later still, when the 'harlequin' ventures once again into the wilderness, he will step literally into another pair of Marlow's shoes (*HD*, p. 103).

31. *The supernatural being*: Proleptic of Kurtz's role. Implicit in this story is the perception of the white man as a god.

32. *a whited sepulchre*: See Matthew 23:27–8: 'Woe unto you, scribes and Pharisees, hypocrites! for ye are like unto whited sepulchres, which indeed appear beautiful outward, but are within full of dead men's bones, and of all uncleanness.' The typescript continues with a more detailed description: 'Its quiet streets empty decorum of its boulevards, all these big houses so intensely respectable to look at and so extremely tight closed suggest the reserve of discreet turpitude.'

33. *the Company's offices*: Conrad was interviewed at 13 rue de Bréderode, Brussels, for his job with the Société Anonyme Belge.

34. *knitting black wool*: Cf. the Fates of Greek legend, Clotho and

Lachesis, who spin the thread of each man's life that is to be cut by Atropos. Dickens had already naturalized them, in *A Tale of Two Cities*, in the persons of Madame Defarge and her companion 'Vengeance', who 'knitted on, with the steadfastness of Fate'.

35. *red . . . blue . . . green . . . orange . . . purple . . . yellow*: Late nineteenth--century maps of the world tended to use a colour code to indicate colonial possessions: red for British territories, blue for French, orange for Portuguese, green for Italian, purple for German and yellow for Belgian.

36. *the jolly lager-beer*: In *Blackwood's Magazine* (June 1898) there was an article by Robert C. Witt, 'An Experiment in Colonization', which described a visit to the German colony in East Africa. Witt recorded how German beer 'flowed as it flows in the Hofbräu at Munich on a hot summer's day' (p. 789).

37. *wisdom*: In the typescript the sentence continues 'as the poor devils went in and out unsuspecting on their way to pit of perdition'.

38. *guarding the door of Darkness*: Cf. the Sibyl in Virgil's *Aeneid*, who guards 'the door of gloomy Dis', i.e., the door of the Underworld into which Aeneas is to descend. See Lillian Feder, 'Marlow's Descent into Hell', *Nineteenth-Century Fiction*, 9.4 (March 1955), pp. 280–92.

39. *Ave! . . . Morituri te salutant*: Marlow quotes the Roman gladiators' salute to the emperor on entering the arena prior to combat: 'Hail! . . . Those who are about to die salute you.' Wallace Watson has suggested that Conrad's use of these words here might derive from the ironic use of them by Maupassant's narrator in his story 'L'Épave' ('"The Shade of Old Flaubert" and Maupassant's "Art impeccable (presque)": French Influences on the Development of Conrad's Marlow', *Journal of Narrative Technique*, 7 (1977), pp. 37–56, especially p. 50.

40. *quoth Plato to his disciples*: Facetious tag.

41. *to measure the crania*: In the late nineteenth century craniology was a flourishing though controversial discipline. Dr Izydor Kopernicki, a leading Polish anthropologist, had asked Conrad in 1881 to assist his craniological studies by collecting skulls during his travels and sending them to a museum in Kraków (Zdzisław Najder [ed.], *Conrad's Polish Background* [London: Oxford University Press, 1964], p. 74).

42. *an alienist*: A person who studies or treats mental illness.

43. *Workers, with a capital*: Cedric Watts compares Thomas Carlyle, *Past and Present* (1843; London: Chapman & Hall, 1858): 'But it is to you, ye Workers, . . . that the whole world calls for new work and nobleness. Subdue mutiny, discord, widespread despair, by manfulness, justice,

mercy and wisdom ... It is work for a God' (p. 302). In 1898 Stanley quoted this passage to justify Leopold II's activities in the Congo: 'Who can doubt that God chose the King for his instrument to redeem this vast slave park' (*Conrad's 'Heart of Darkness': A Critical and Contextual Discussion* [Milan: Mursia International, 1977], p. 60).

44. *sort of apostle*: In 1882 the French press had described the explorer Pierre de Brazza as an 'apostle of liberty' who had dealt 'a death blow to slavery in West Africa'.

45. *such rot*: Consider, for example, the speech with which King Leopold II of Belgium opened his geographical conference on Central Africa in September 1876: 'To open to civilization the only part of our globe where it has yet to penetrate, to pierce the darkness which envelops whole populations, it is, I dare to say, a crusade worthy of this century of progress' (Thomas Pakenham, *The Scramble for Africa* [Weidenfeld & Nicolson, 1991; Abacus 1992], p. 21). As Pakenham suggests, Leopold's attention had been drawn to Central Africa by a report in *The Times* (11 January 1876) headed 'African Exploration', which described the interior of Africa as 'a magnificent and healthy country of unspeakable richness' that would 'repay any enterprising capitalist that might take the matter in hand' (p. 12).

46. *worthy of his hire*: Luke 10:7.

47. *the centre of the earth*: For a detailed discussion of *Heart of Darkness* in relation to Jules Verne's *Voyage au centre de la terre*, see Graham Huggan, 'Voyages towards an Absent Centre', the *Conradian*, 14.1/2 (December 1989), pp. 19–46.

48. *in a French steamer*: In the manuscript Conrad writes after this 'and beginning with Dakar'. As Norman Sherry pointed out, the *Ville de Maceio*, in which Conrad travelled from Bordeaux in 1890, made its first stop at Tenerife. It subsequently called at Dakar, Conakry, Freetown, Grand Bassam on the Ivory Coast, Grand Popo in Dahomey, Libreville and, finally, Banana, before moving up Banana Creek to Boma (Sherry, p. 23).

49. *one of their wars*: Between March and October 1890 the French attempted to conquer the African kingdom of Dahomey.

50. *dropped limp*: This is the reading of all texts except the manuscript and the Heinemann, which give 'drooped limp'.

51. *eight-inch guns*: From ten-inch in the manuscript, these became eight-inch in typescript, serial and first-edition texts, and six-inch in the Dent and Heinemann texts.

52. *he called them enemies*: For a discussion of linguistic self-consciousness in *Heart of Darkness*, see Jeremy Hawthorn, *Joseph Conrad: Language and Fictional Self-consciousness* (London: Edward Arnold, 1979), pp. 7–36.

53. *the seat of the government*: Boma. In the manuscript there now follows a detailed description of Boma's hotel, foreshore, tramway and government. (See 'Introduction', n. 29).

54. *a Swede*: There was a Swedish captain, Axel Tjulin, on the lower Congo between June and December 1890 (Sherry, p. 398).

55. *At last*: In both manuscript and typescript there is a slightly fuller account of the journey on board the steamer before this.

56. *Company's station*: Matadi.

57. *building a railway*: Stanley had argued that the economic success of the Congo Free State depended on building a railway to bypass the cataracts. In 1887 Albert Thys had surveyed the route for the railway, and in 1889 the Compagnie du Chemin de Fer was set up. The first rails and sleepers were actually brought out on the *Ville de Maceio* in May 1890 with Conrad. The railway, due to be completed in 1894, wasn't actually completed until 1898.

58. *the gloomy circle of some Inferno*: An allusion to the topography of Hell in Dante's *Inferno*.

59. *had withdrawn to die*: Louis Goffin's *Le Chemin de fer du Congo* (Brussels: Weissenbruch, 1907) emphasizes the high mortality rate among the black workers during the construction of the railway through the Congo and notes how they often withdrew into the bush to die.

60. *a clear silk necktie*: This began as a 'silk necktie' in the manuscript (with the word 'clear' inserted later before 'silk'); it appears as 'a clear necktie' in the 1902 edition and as 'a clean necktie' in the Heinemann text.

61. *apple-pie order*: In the manuscript there is a deleted reference at this point to Marlow being introduced to the station either 'with the English chaplain' or (as Sherry reads it) 'as the English captain'.

62. *Mr Kurtz*: When Conrad reached Stanley Falls in September 1890 in the *Roi des Belges*, the vessel took on board an agent of the company, Georges Antoine Klein, who died of dysentery during the voyage downstream. In the manuscript Conrad began by writing 'Monsieur Klein'; this was changed to 'Mr Klein', and then 'Klein' was cancelled after the fourth time and replaced by Kurtz. 'Klein' is German for 'small', as 'Kurz' is German for 'short'.

63. *The population had cleared out*: In his book *Pioneering in the Congo* (London: Religious Tract Society, 1900), W. Holman Bentley reveals that this was quite a common phenomenon ('Sometimes they would find the birds flown – the village empty', pp. 42–3), the reason given being a fear of Arab slave-raids.

64. *bells in a Christian country:* Marlow might be closer to the truth than he realizes. Bentley notes that Ntotela, 'King of Congo', ordered drums to be beaten at San Salvador (now in Angola) on Saturday night and Sunday morning to announce the Christian church service (I, 136).

65. *Zanzibaris*: The natives of Zanzibar were used as mercenaries throughout Africa; they were also involved in the slave trade.

66. *a white companion*: For this part of his journey Conrad had a European companion, Prosper Harou, who, like Marlow's companion, was stricken with fever and had to be carried in a hammock. See *The Congo Diary* p. 159. Prosper Harou's older brother had accompanied Stanley on his 1879–82 Congo expedition.

67. *the Central Station*: That is, Kinshasa. The manager of the station when Conrad was there was Camille Delcommune.

68. *I see it now*: Before Conrad reached Kinshasa at the beginning of August 1890, he heard that the *Florida*, which he had expected to command, was wrecked. (See *The Congo Diary*, p. 158). Conrad has used this detail as part of what Cedric Watts calls a 'covert plot' (*The Deceptive Text: An Introduction to Covert Plots*, pp. 119–20). However, as Sherry points out, the *Florida* was wrecked, salvaged and brought back to Kinshasa by 23 July: Conrad was not, like Marlow, delayed there for three months and involved in the salvage work (Sherry, pp. 40–41).

69. *round table*: Cf. King Arthur's round table at Camelot.

70. *faithless pilgrims*: Cf. John Bunyan's *The Pilgrim's Progress*. Marlow gives the traders this name because of the 'long staves' they carry.

71. *a forked little beard and a hooked nose*: Cf. the traditional representation of the devil.

72. *straw maybe*: Proverbial.

73. *An act of special creation*: Marlow playfully alludes to a non-evolutionist explanation for the existence of such creatures as the apteryx of New Zealand and the red grouse of England.

74. *at a halter*: A witty variant on the proverb, 'One man may steal a horse, while another may not look over a hedge.'

75. *worth his while*: In earlier versions, from the manuscript through to the serial version, there was an additional sentence here: 'His allusions were Chinese to me.'

76. *carrying a lighted torch*: Astraea, goddess of justice, is often depicted as blindfolded (to signify the impartiality of justice), while Liberty is depicted as bearing a lighted torch. Kurtz's image is more disturbing and less easily interpreted. Earlier the primary narrator had referred to English explorers and adventurers as bearers of 'the torch', 'bearers of a spark from the sacred fire' (p. 17), Marlow, by contrast, referred to the Romans in Africa as 'men going at it blind' (p. 20).

77. *Mephistopheles*: The diabolic agent of Lucifer. See Goethe's *Faust*.

78. *an ichthyosaurus*: A prehistoric reptile.

79. *Eldorado*: In 'Geography and Some Explorers' Conrad observes:

I suppose it is not very charitable of me, but I must say that to this day I feel a malicious pleasure at the many disappointments of those pertinaceous searchers for El Dorado who climbed mountains, pushed through forests, swam rivers, floundered in bogs, without giving a single thought to the science of geography. Not for them the serene joys of scientific research, but infinite toil, in hunger, thirst, sickness, battle; with broken heads, unseemly squabbles, and empty pockets in the end (*LE* p. 5).

80. *Expedition*: Alexandre Delcommune's Katanga expedition arrived at Kinshasa in three instalments on 20, 23 September and 5 October 1890; they left on 17 October.

81. '*Make rain and fine weather*': In 'Frazer, Conrad and the "truth of primitive passion"', I have suggested that this utterance is one of a number in the story that collectively relate Kurtz to the type of man–god whom Frazer called 'weather king'. See Robert Fraser (ed.), *Sir James Frazer and the Literary Imagination* (Basingstoke: Macmillan, 1990), pp. 172–91. In *The Golden Bough* (London: Macmillan, 1890), Frazer notes that 'Weather kings are common in Africa' (I, 44) and cites the Banjars of West Africa as ascribing to their king 'the power of causing rain or fine weather' (I, 47). Another of his examples of a 'rain-maker' is 'Namvulu Vumu, King of the Rain and Storm', who lives 'on a hill at Bomma (the mouth of the Congo)' (I, 52). W. Holman Bentley notes: 'These poor inland folk believe that we are gods, that we send the rain, and can withhold it at will' (*Pioneering in the Congo*, I, 313).

82. *conceive you*: A Gallicism, perhaps to indicate that this dialogue takes place in French.

83. *twenty cannibals*: Sherry notes that the crews of Congo steamers were

'from the upper Congo, mainly from Bangala' and suggests that the Bangalas were 'joyfully cannibalistic' (Sherry, p. 59).

84. *three or four pilgrims*: In the *Roi des Belges*, Conrad was accompanied by Camille Delcommune, Captain Koch, three agents (Keyaerts, Rollin and Vander Heyden) and a mechanic (Gossen).

85. *exclusively*: In the manuscript there appears at this point the sentence 'Towards the man possessed of moral ideas holding a torch in the heart of darkness.'

86. *war, peace, or prayer*: Compare with Bentley's account of his first journey to Kinshasa in 1881: 'We had heard drums before, but until now had not thought much of them. From this time they became an intolerable nuisance. As we passed along, one town would beat a warning to the next' (I, 315).

87. *strips of woollen blanket*: This is part of the novella's complicated system of echoes. As Frances B. Singh points out, 'the physical manifestation of [Marlow's] devotion to his job, the strips of woolen blanket hastily tied to leaky steam-pipes, looks perilously similar to his "very second-rate" helmsman's impromptu magic "charm, made of rags, tied to his arm"' ('The Colonialistic Bias of *Heart of Darkness*', *Conradiana*, 10.1 [1978], pp. 41–54).

88. *a vertical boiler*: A cylindrical boiler with a vertical firebox.

89. *some such name*: J.A. Arnold has suggested that Marlow or Conrad linked the name of J.T. Towson to a book by Nicholas Tinmouth. J.T. Towson published two volumes of navigation tables (in 1848 and 1849), but he did not publish a handbook on points of seamanship. Nicholas Tinmouth, on the other hand, published *An Inquiry Relative to Various Important Points of Seamanship, Considered as a Branch of Practical Science* in 1845. The opening chapters inquired 'earnestly into the breaking strain of ships' chains and tackle', and the book also contains the 'illustrative diagrams' and 'repulsive tables of figures' mentioned by Marlow, but Tinmouth was not a 'Master in his Majesty's Navy' – he was a Master-Attendant at Her Majesty's Dockyard at Woolwich. See J.A. Arnold, 'The Young Russian's Book in Conrad's *Heart of Darkness*', *Conradiana*, 7.2 (1976), pp. 121–6. In *The Political Novels of Joseph Conrad* (Chicago: University of Chicago Press, 1963) Eloise Knapp Hay suggests A.H. Alston's *Seamanship and Its Associated Duties* (1860), which she described as 'one of Conrad's favorite books', as a possible source (p. 144).

90. *a state of trance*: Cf. the enchanted forest of 'Sleeping Beauty'.

91. *eight hundred miles away*: The Bangalas lived about 900 miles from the mouth of the Congo.

92. *nine inches long*: J. Rose Troup, in *With Stanley's Rear Column* (London: Chapman & Hall, 1890), records that brass rods (*mitakos*) were 'the currency among the natives at Leopoldville and most of the regions of the Upper Congo' (p. 103).

93. *like half-cooked dough*: This is *kwanga*, i.e., manioc or tapioca, steeped and boiled to form a stiff dough.

94. *a fabulous castle*: Cf. 'Sleeping Beauty'.

95. *a decked scow*: A large, flat-bottomed boat.

96. *Martini-Henry*: A breech-action military rifle. (These became army issue around 1875.)

97. *the steam-whistle*: Bentley records an incident during a journey on the Kwangu, a tributary of the Congo, when four men in a canoe tried to levy a toll on the steamship: 'They demanded blackmail, and lay across our bows. The two whistles of the *Peace* shrieked their loudest . . . There was an instant collapse in the canoe; guns were dropped and paddles were seized and plied to their utmost' (II, 139).

98. *the hair goes on growing*: That is, on corpses. (Marlow has just referred to 'the disinterred body of Mr Kurtz'.)

99. *his father was half-French*: Conrad notes 'I took great care to give Kurtz a cosmopolitan origin' (Frederick Karl and Laurence Davies [eds.], *The Collected Letters of Joseph Conrad*, [Cambridge: Cambridge University Press, 1988], III, p. 94; hereafter cited as *CLJC*). See 'Introduction', pp. xx–xxi.

100. *International Society for the Suppression of Savage Customs*: Conrad might have had in mind the International Association for the Exploration and Civilizing of Africa (Association Internationale pour l'Exploration et la Civilisation en Afrique), of which King Leopold was the president.

101. *a harlequin*: First found in French folk literature, as a ragamuffin of demoniacal appearance and character; later, one of the figures in the Italian *Commedia dell'arte*; subsequently appeared in English pantomime as an acrobatic character, dressed in a particoloured costume.

102. *blue, red, and yellow*: Perhaps an echo of the map of the world with its colour-coding for colonies.

103. *Government of Tambov*: Tambov, at this time, was one of the largest governments of Central Russia; one of its chief towns, also called Tambov, was an archiepiscopal see of the Greek Orthodox Church.

104. *a Dutch trading-house on the coast*: The Nieuwe Afrikaansche

Handelsvennootschap (or Dutch Trading Company). According to Bentley, in the 1870s this was the most powerful company on the coast and on the river (I, 69).

105. *old Van Shuyten*: Schuyten is a more likely spelling for a Dutch name. Sherry suggests that Conrad took the name from Schouten, a Belgian associated with Hodister (Sherry, p. 117).

106. *those heads on the stakes*: Sherry notes that the station at Yanga was decorated with human heads (Sherry, p. 118). Similarly, when Delcommune's expedition reached Katanga in April 1891, they were entertained by Msiri in a compound surrounded by trees from which hung a collection of human skulls.

107. *mostly fossil*: That is, it has been buried in the ground.

108. *A black figure*: Contrary to Chinua Achebe's reading, this figure is 'black' because it is silhouetted against the fire. Nevertheless, the scene – with horned figures and fire – clearly suggests the satanic.

109. *struggled with a soul*: In *Joseph Conrad's Bible* (Norman, Oklahoma: University of Oklahoma Press, 1984) Dwight H. Purdy compares this scene to Jacob wrestling with the Angel (Genesis 32).

110. *fierce river-demon*: The trope is a conventional way of suggesting 'primitive' animistic interpretations of European technology, but it has an ironic relation to Marlow's own demonizing of the Africans.

111. *kings meet him at railway-stations*: When Stanley arrived at Marseilles Railway Station (on 8 January 1878) after completing a journey across Africa from Zanzibar to Boma, he was met by emissaries from Leopold II. See 'Introduction', pp. xix–xx.

112. *'The horror! The horror!'*: As Cedric Watts observes in his edition of *Heart of Darkness*, this exclamation is probably the most famous Conradian crux: not only have different critics offered different readings of it, but Marlow himself offers a range of interpretations. Watts provides a succinct summary of Marlow's shifting interpretations of 'The horror!': (a) that Kurtz is passing a moral judgement on his own actions, and that this 'judgement upon the adventures of his soul' is 'an affirmation, a moral victory'; (b) that Kurtz's judgement of his actions is more ambivalent, condemning his actions but also registering the temptation (his whisper has 'the strange commingling of desire and hate'); (c) that Kurtz is passing judgement on human nature ('no eloquence could have been so withering to one's belief in mankind as his final burst of sincerity'); (d) that Kurtz is passing judgement on all existence ('that wide and immense stare embracing, condemning, loathing all the universe'). In each case we are dealing with Marlow's interpretation of Kurtz's interpretation of his experiences. If the utterance acts, as Watts suggests, as 'a thematic nexus', it does not provide an 'answer' so much as involve us in Marlow's efforts to interpret his Congo experience and plunge us into the multi-layered indeterminacies of the novella.

113. *I had peeped over the edge*: Cf. Edgar Allan Poe's story, 'A Descent into the Maelström'.

114. *a danger it is unable to comprehend*: Cf. the end of H.G. Wells's *The Island of Dr Moreau*.

115. *some other feeling perhaps*: Conrad told David Meldrum that *Heart of Darkness* offered 'A mere shadow of love interest just in the last pages' (*CLJC*, II, pp. 145–6).

116. *out of the glassy panel*: Cf. Dickens's *A Christmas Carol*, where Marley's face similarly confronts Scrooge as he faces a door. However, the face Marlow sees in the 'glassy panel' is also his own reflection.

117. *The heavens do not fall*: Marlow is recalling the Latin maxim, 'Fiat justitia, ruat coelum' ('Let justice be done, though the heavens fall'), which Conrad had quoted in a letter to Marguerite Poradowska in March 1890, shortly before he set out for the Congo (*CLJC*, I, p. 43).

THE CONGO DIARY

THE CONGO DIARY MAP

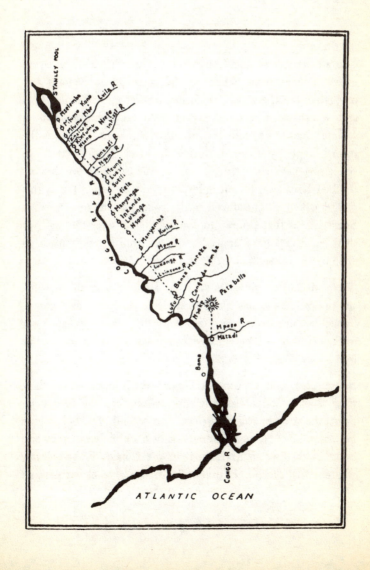

NOTE ON THE TEXT

Conrad arrived in the Congo on 12 June 1890. The thirty miles of river from Boma on the coast up to Matadi was navigable, but the 230-mile journey further up to Stanley Pool and Kinshasa, where he expected to take command of a steamer, had to be made across land. *The Congo Diary* was the record kept by Conrad during his trek from Matadi to Nselemba between 13 June and 1 August. (He presumably reached Kinshasa, fifteen miles away, on 2 August.) It is this record which is reproduced in the pages that follow. Norman Sherry notes that Conrad took much longer over this journey than he should have done. He quotes from a report made in 1888 by the missionary G.W. Brourke:

[From Matadi] a road leaves the river, or rather a narrow footpath, and runs across the hills, along rocky ridges, down into deep gorges, through rushing streams, up steep slopes, over sandy plateaux away to Stanley Pool – about 17 days continuous marching for a white man . . . (*Conrad's Western World*, p. 36)

Subsequently, in a second notebook, which he called his 'Up-river Book', Conrad recorded his journey up the Congo on board the steamer *Roi des Belges*. This second notebook, which he began on 3 August, contains almost exclusively notes and sketches relating to navigating up the Congo. It was clearly written with the purely practical purpose of assisting Conrad when navigating the steamer on some future up-river trip, and it is not reproduced here.

The manuscripts of the two notebooks are both in the Houghton Library, Harvard University. Richard Curle first published an edited and annotated version of *The Congo Diary* in the English shipping magazine *The Blue Peter* (volume 5, October 1925, pp. 319–25), which he later republished in his edition of Conrad's *Last Essays* (London: J.M. Dent, 1926). More recently Józef Miłobędzki published his annotated and generally accurate transcription of both notebooks in the Polish quarterly *Nautologia* (volume 1, dated 1972, published 1974), and Zdzisław Najder published a slightly less accurate transcription of both texts in his volume *Congo Diary and Other Uncollected Pieces* (Garden City, New York: Doubleday, 1978). I have compared the texts published by Curle, Miłobędzki and Najder with the manuscript, and I have drawn on, supplemented and corrected the annotations each has made.

The notebook containing *The Congo Diary* continues with several more pages of notes and drawings after the last of the diary entries. Some of these were made on board the *Torrens* two years later. Three pages, however, consist of English and French words and phrases translated into Kikongo; there are further listings of Congo markets; and there are a couple of Congo addresses 'Lukunga – Mr Hoste' and 'Banza Manteka – Mr Ingham'. One page notes the titles of four works: C.M. Woodford's *A Naturalist among the Head-Hunters, being an account of three visits to the Solomon Islands in the years 1886, 1887 and 1888* (1890), Clement Markham's *John Davis: Arctic Explorer and Early India Navigator* (1891), James Grant's *The Newspaper Press: Its Origin, Progress and Present Position* (1871), and Arthur Palmer's 'A Battle Described from the Ranks', *The Nineteenth Century* (March 1890), pp. 397–407. These pages are not included here.

The 'rough map' accompanied Richard Curle's publication of the diary in both magazine and book form. Not all of the place-names in Conrad's diary were accurately transcribed by Curle, and he reproduced the errors in his map. There are therefore discrepancies between the map and *The Congo Diary* text published here. Conrad's spelling ('andulating', 'ressembling'), punctuation and inconsistent abbreviations have been reproduced and not standardized.

The Congo Diary

Abbreviations

acquain^{ce}: acquaintance
after^{ds}: afterwards
av^{ge}: average
camp^{g}: camping
camp^{g}: camping
com^{al}: commercial
compy: company
dist^{ce}: distance
E^{d}: eastward
est^{d}: estimated
gov^{t}: government
gov^{t}: government
H.: Harou
missio.: missionaries
mket: market
Nth: north
offer: officer
sta^{on}: station
Sth: south
v.g.: very good

Arrived at Matadi[1] on the 13th of June 1890. –

Mr Gosse[2] chief of the station (O.K.) retaining us for some reason of his own.

Made the acquaintance of Mr Roger Casement,[3] which I should consider as a great pleasure under any circumstances and now it becomes a positive piece of luck.

Thinks, speaks well, most intelligent and very sympathetic. –

Feel considerably in doubt about the future. Think just now that my life amongst the people (white) around here can not be very comfortable. Intend avoid acquaintances as much as possible.

Through Mr R.C. Have made the acquain^{ce} of Mr Underwood the manager of the English factory (Hatton & Cookson, in Kalla Kalla. Av^{ge} com^{al} – Hearty and kind. Lunched there on the 21st. –

24th Gosse and R.C. gone with a large lot of ivory down to Boma. On G. return intend to start up the river. Have been myself busy packing ivory in casks.[4] Idiotic employment. Health good up to now.

Wrote to Simpson,[5] to Gov.B.[6] to Purd.[7] to Hope,[8] to Cap Froud,[9] and to Mar.[10] Prominent characteristic of the social life here: People speaking ill of each other.[11] –

Saturday 28th June left Matadi with Mr Harou[12] and a

caravan of 31 men. Parted with Casement in a very friendly manner. Mr Gosse saw us off as far as the State station. –

First halt. M'poso. 2 Danes in Compny.[13]

Sund. 29th. Ascent of Palaballa. Sufficiently fatiguing – Camped at 11[h] am at Nsoke-River.[14] Mosquitos.

Monday. 30th to Congo da Lemba[15] after passing black rocks long ascent. Harou giving up. Bother. Camp bad. Water far. Dirty. At night Harou better.

1st <u>July.</u>
<u>Tuesday.</u> 1st. Left early in a heavy mist marching towards Lufu River. – Part route through forest on the sharp slope of a high mountain. Very long descent. Then, market place,[16] from where short walk to the bridge[17] (good) and camp. V.G. Bath. Clear river. Feel well Harou all right. 1st chicken. <u>2p.</u>[m]

No sunshine to day –

<u>Wednesday</u> 2[d] July –
Started at 5[h] 30 after a sleepless night. Country more open – Gently andulating hills. Road good in perfect order. (District of Lukungu). Great market[18] at 9.30. bought eggs & chickens –

Feel not well to day. Heavy cold in the head. Arrived at 11[h] at Banza Manteka.[19] Camped on the market place. Not well enough to call on the missionary. Water scarce and bad – Camp[g] place dirty. –

2 Danes still in company

Thursday 3[d] July.
Left at 6am. after a good night's rest. Crossed a low range of hills and entered a broad valley or rather plain with a break

in the middle – Met an offer of the State inspecting. A few
minutes afterwards saw at a camp^g place[20] the dead body of
a Backongo. Shot?[21] Horrid smell. – Crossed a range of
mountains running NW-SE. by a low pass. Another broad
flat valley with a deep ravine through the centre. – Clay
and gravel. Another range parallel to the first-mentioned
with a chain of low foothills running close to it. Between
the two came to camp on the banks of Luinzono River.[22]
Camp^g place clean. River clear. Gov^t. Zanzibari with register.[23] Canoe. 2 danes camp^g on the other bank. –
Health good.

 General tone of landscape grey yellowish (Dry grass) with
reddish patches (Soil) and clumps of dark green vegetation
scattered sparsely about. Mostly in steep gorges between the
higher mountains or in ravines cutting the plain[24] – Noticed
Palma Christi – Oil palm. Very straight tall and thick trees in
some places. Name not known to me. Villages quite invisible.
Infer their existence from calbashes suspended to palm trees
for the 'malafu'.[25] –

Good many caravans and travellers. No women unless on
the market place. –

Bird notes charming – One especially a flute-like note.
Another kind of 'boom' ressembling the very distant baying of
a hound. – Saw only pigeons and a few green parroquets; very
small and not many No birds of prey seen by me. Up to 9am –
sky clouded and calm – Afterwards gentle breeze from the Nth
generally and sky clearing – Nights damp and cool. – White
mists on the hills up about halfway. Water effects, very
beautiful this morning. Mists generally raising before sky
clears.

[A sketch entitled 'Section of to day's road.' Marked on the
sketch: 'Banza Manteka, 3 hills and Luinzono River'. Beneath

the sketch: 'Distance 15 miles. General direction NNE-SSW'.]

Friday – 4th July. –
Left camp at 6^h am – after a very unpleasant night – Marching across a chain of hills and then in a maze of hills – At 8.15 opened out into an andulating plain Took bearings of a break in the chain of mountains on the other side – Bearing <u>NNE</u> – Road passes through that Sharp ascents up very steep hills not very high. The higher mountains recede sharply and show a low hilly country –

At 9.30 Market place.²⁶

At 10^h passed R. Lukanga and at 10.30 Camped on the Mpwe R.²⁷

[A sketch entitled: 'To day's march'. Underneath title: 'Direction NNE½N Distce 13 miles'. Marked on sketch: 'Luinzono, Camp'.]

Saw another dead body lying by the path in an attitude of meditative repose. –

In the evening 3 women of whom one albino passed our camp – Horrid chalky white with pink blotches. Red eyes. Red hair. Features very negroid and ugly. –

Mosquitos. At night when the moon rose heard shouts and drumming in distant villages²⁸ Passed a bad night.

Saturday 5th July. 90.
Left at 6.15. Morning cool, even cold and very damp – Sky densely overcast. Gentle breeze from NE. Road through a narrow plain up to R. <u>Kwilu</u>. Swift flowing and deep 50 yds wide – Passed in canoes – After^{ds} up and down very steep hills intersected by deep ravines – Main chain of heights running mostly NW-SE or W and E at times. Stopped at Manyamba²⁹

– Camp^g place bad – in a hollow – Water very indifferent. Tent set at 10$^{\underline{h}}$ 15$^{\underline{m}}$

[A sketch entitled: 'Section of to day's road'. Underneath title: 'NNE Dist$^{\underline{ce}}$ 12$^{\underline{m}}$. Marked on sketch: 'Kwilu River, Camp Manyamba'.]

To day fell into a muddy puddle. Beastly. The fault of the man that carried me. After camp^g went to a small stream bathed and washed clothes. – Getting jolly well sick of this fun. –

Tomorrow expect a long march to get to Nsona.[30] 2 days from Manyanga. –

No sunshine to-day.

Sunday 6th July –

Started at 5.40. – the route at first hilly then after a sharp descent traversing a broad plain. At the end of it a large market place[31]

At 10$^{\underline{h}}$ sun came out. –

After leaving the market passed another plain then walking on the crest of a chain of hills passed 2 villages[32] and at 11^h arrived at Nsona. – Village invisible –

[A sketch entitled: 'Section of day's march'. Sketch marked: 'Market, Camp Nsona'. Underneath: 'Direction about NNE Distance – 18 miles'.]

In this camp (Nsona –) there is a good camp^{g}place Shady. Water far and not very good. – This night no mosquitos owing to large fires lit all round our tent. –

Afternoon very close

Night clear and starry.

Monday-7th July. –

Left at ·6$^{\underline{h}}$ after a good night's rest on the road to Inkandu[33] which is some distance past Lukungu gov$^{\underline{t}}$ station. –

Route very accidented.[34] Succession of round steep hills. At times walking along the crest of a chain of hills. –

Just before Lukunga our carriers took a wide sweep to the southward till the station bore Nth. – Walking through long grass for 1½ hours. – Crossed a broad river about 100 feet wide and 4 deep. – After another ½ hours walk through manioc plantations[35] in good order rejoined our route to the E$^{\underline{d}}$ of the Lukunga Sta$^{\underline{on}}$ Walking along an undulating plain towards the Inkandu market on a hill. – Hot, thirsty and tired. At 11^h arrived on the mketplace – About 200 people. – Business brisk. No water. No camp^g place – After remaining for one hour left in search of a resting place. –

Row with carriers. – No water. At last about 1½ p.m. camped on an exposed hill side near a muddy creek. No shade. Tent on a slope. Sun heavy. Wretched.

[Untitled sketch of day's journey. Marked on sketch: 'Nsona, Lukunga, River bearing Nth, Inkandu, Camp'. Underneath: 'Direction NE by N. Distance 22 miles'.]

Night miserably cold.

No sleep. Mosquitos –

Tuesday 8th July

Left at 6$^{\underline{h}}$ am

About ten minutes from camp left main gov^t path for the Manyanga track. Sky overcast. Road up and down all the time – Passing a couple of villages

The country presents a confused wilderness of hills land slips on their sides showing red. Fine effect of red hill covered in places by dark green vegetation

½ hour before beginning the descent got a glimpse of the Congo. – Sky clouded.

[A sketch entitled: 'To day's march – 3$^{\underline{h}}$'. Marked on sketch: 'Camp, River, Hill, Congo, Manyanga'. Underneath: 'NbyE← SbyW General direction NbyE Dist$\underline{^{ce}}$ 9$\frac{1}{2}$ miles'.]

Arrived at Manyanga at 9$\underline{^h}$ a.m.

Received most kindly by Messrs Heyn & Jaeger.[36] –

Most comfortable and pleasant halt. –

Stayed here till the 25.[37] Both have been sick. – Most kindly care taken of us. Leave with sincere regret.

(Mafiela)

Frid^y 25th –	Nkenghe	–	<u>left</u>
Sat. 26	Nsona		Nkendo K
Sund. 27	Nkandu		<u>Luasi</u>
Mond 28	Nkonzo		<u>Nzungi</u> (Ngoma)
Tues. 29	Nkenghe		Inkissi
Wedn: 30	Nsona	<u>mercredi</u> –	Stream
Thurs: 31.	Nkandu		Luila
Frid^y 1st Aug.	Nkonzo		Nselemba
Sat$^{\underline{y}}$ 2^d	Nkenghe		
Sund. 3^d	Nsona		
Mond. 4th	Nkandu		
Tues^d: 5th	Nkonzo.		
Wedn$^{\underline{y}}$ 6th	Nkenghe.[38]		

<u>Friday the 25th July 1890.</u> –

Left Manyanga at 2$\frac{1}{2}$ p.m – with plenty of hammock carriers. H. lame and not in very good form. Myself ditto but not lame. Walked as far as Mafiela and camped – 2$\underline{^h}$

Saturday – 26th

Left very early – Road ascending all the time. – Passed villages. Country seems thickly inhabited. At 11$\underline{^h}$ arrived at large Market place.[39] Left at noon and camped at 1^h pm.

[Untitled sketch of day's journey marked: 'Mafiela, Croco-dile pond, mount, govt path, market, a white man died here, camp'. Underneath: 'General direction E$\frac{1}{2}$N ← W$\frac{1}{2}$S. / Sun visible at 8 am. very hot / distance – 18 miles'.]

Sunday. 27th
Left at 8[h] am. Sent luggage carriers straight on to Luasi and went ourselves round by the Mission of Sutili.

Hospitable reception by Mrs Comber[40] – all the missio. absent. –

The looks of the whole establishment eminently civilized and very refreshing to see after the lots of tumble down hovels in which the state & company agents are content to live. –

Fine buildings. Position on a hill. Rather breezy. –

Left at 3[h] pm. At the first heavy ascent met Mr Davis Miss.[41] returning from a preaching trip. Rev. Bentley[42] away in the south with his wife. –

This being off the road no section given – Distance traversed about 15 miles – Gen. Direction E N E. –

At Luasi we get on again on to the gov[t] road. –

Camped at 4$\frac{1}{2}$ pm. with Mr Heche in company. –

To day no sunshine –

Wind remarkably cold –

Gloomy day. –

Monday. 28th
Left camp at 6.30 after breakfasting with Heche –

Road at first hilly. Then walking along the ridges of hill chains with valleys on both sides. – The country more open and there is much more trees[43] growing in large clumps in the ravines. –

Passed Nzungi[44] and camped 11[h] on the right bank of

Ngoma. A rapid little river with rocky bed. Village on a hill to the right. –

[Untitled sketch marked: 'Camp, Luasi, River, Ridge, Wooded valleys, Nzungi, Ngoma River, Camp'. Underneath: 'General direction ENE/Distance – 14 miles'.]

No sunshine. Gloomy cold day. Squalls.

Tuesday – 29th
Left camp at 7[h] after a good night's rest. Continuous ascent; rather easy at first. – Crossed wooded ravines and the river Lunzadi by a very decent bridge[45] –

At 9[h] met Mr Louette escorting a sick agent of the Comp[y] back to Matadi – Looking very well – Bad news from up the river – All the steamers disabled. One wrecked.[46] – Country wooded – At 10.30 camped at Inkissi

[Untitled sketch marked: 'Ngoma, Lunzadi River, Met Mr Louette, Inkissi River, Camp'. Underneath: 'General direction ENE/Distce 15 miles'.]

Sun visible at 6.30. Very warm day. –

29th
Inkissi River very rapid, is about 100 yards broad – Passage in canoes. – Banks wooded very densely and valley of the river rather deep but very narrow. –

To day did not set the tent but put up in gov[t] shimbek.[47] Zanzibari in charge – Very obliging. – Met ripe pineapple for the first time. –

On the road to day passed a skeleton tied-up to a post. Also white man's grave – No name. heap of stones in the form of a cross.

Health good now –

Wednesday – 30th.

Left at 6 am intending to camp at Kinfumu – Two hours sharp walk brought me to Nsona na Nsefe – Market – $\frac{1}{2}$ hour after Harou arrived very ill with billious attack and fever. – Laid him down in gov^t shimbek – Dose of Ipeca.[48] Vomiting bile in enormous quantities. At 11^h gave him 1 gramme of quinine and lots of hot tea. Hot fit ending in heavy perspiration. At 9^h p.m. put him in hammock and started for Kinfumu – Row with carriers all the way.[49] Harou suffering much through the jerks of the hammock Camped at a small stream. –

At 4^h Harou better. Fever gone. –

[Untitled sketch marked: 'Sward, A remarkable conical mountain bearing NE visible from here, Wood, Lulufu River, Open, Wood, Stream, Nsona a Nsefe, Grass, Camp, Wooded'. Underneath: 'General direction NEbyE$\frac{1}{2}$E –/Distance 13 miles –']

Up till noon, sky clouded and strong NW wind very chilling. From 1^h pm to 4^h pm sky clear and very hot day. Expect lots of battles with carriers to-morrow – Had them all called and made a speech which they did not understand.[50] They promise good behaviour

Thursday – 31st

Left at 6^h – Sent Harou ahead and followed in $\frac{1}{2}$ an hour. – Road presents several sharp ascents and a few others easier but rather long. Notice in places sandy surface soil instead of hard clay as heretofore; think however that the layer of sand is not very thick and that the clay would be found under it. Great difficulty in carrying Harou. – Too heavy. Bother! Made two long halts to rest the carriers. Country wooded in valleys and on many of the ridges.

[A sketch entitled: 'Section of to-day's road'. Sketch marked:

'Camp, Nkenghe, Kinfumu River, Congo, Kinzilu River, Luila River, and NE½E'.]

At 2.30 pm reached Luila at last and camped on right bank. – Breeze from SW

General direction of march about NE½E

Distance est$\underline{d}$ – 16 miles

Congo very narrow and rapid. Kinzilu rushing in. A short distance up from the mouth fine waterfall. –

– Sun rose red – From 9^h a.m. infernally hot day. –

Harou very little better.

Self rather seedy. Bathed.

Luila about 60 feet wide. Shallow

Friday – 1$^{\underline{st}}$ of August 1890

Left at 6.30 am after a very indifferently passed night – Cold, Heavy mists – Road in long ascents and sharp dips all the way to Mfumu Mbé –

After leaving there a long and painful climb up a very steep hill; then a long descent to Mfumu Koko where a long halt was made.

Left at 12.30pm – towards Nselemba. Many ascents – The aspect of the country entirely changed – Wooded hills with openings. – Path almost all the afternoon thro a forest of light trees with dense undergrowth. –

After a halt on a wooded hillside reached Nselemba at 4^h 10^m pm.

[Untitled sketch of day's march marked: 'Camp, Mfumu Mbe, Koko, Stream, Stream, Mostly Wooded, Stream, Nselemba, and Camp'.]

Put up at gov^t shanty. –

Row between the carriers and a man stating himself in gov^t employ, about a mat. – Blows with sticks raining hard – Stopped it. Chief came with a youth about 13 suffering from gunshot wound in the head. Bullet entered about an inch above the right eyebrow and came out a little inside the roots of the hair, fairly in the middle of the brow in a line with the bridge of the nose – Bone not damaged apparently. Gave him a little glycerine to put on the wound made by the bullet on coming out.

Harou not very well. Mosquitos – Frogs – Beastly. Glad to see the end of this stupid tramp. Feel rather seedy.

Sun rose red – Very hot day – Wind Sth.

General direction of march – NEbyN

Distance about   17 miles

NOTES ON *THE CONGO DIARY*

In compiling these notes, I have been able (thanks to the generosity of Hans van Marle) to draw on the contemporary itinerary for Belgian State Officials for the journey from Matadi to Nselemba: *Carte des route de portage dans le région des chutes du Congo dressée par le lieutenant Louis chef de bureau à l'État du Congo* [1894]. I am very grateful to Hans van Marle for making this available to me and for other assistance with annotation.

1. *Matadi*: An important centre of trade about thirty miles upstream from Boma at the mouth of the Congo, inhabited at this time by well over one hundred Europeans. (See map, p. 143.)
2. *Mr Gosse*: Joseph-Louis-Herbert Gosse had recently been made manager of the Matadi Station of the Société Anonyme Belge pour le Commerce du Haut-Congo.
3. *Mr Roger Casement*: (1864–1916) at this period was working for the Compagnie du Chemin de Fer du Congo as a supervisor of the railway that was planned to connect Matadi with Kinshasa; in 1898 he became British Consul for the Congo Free State; in 1903 he prepared a widely publicized report on atrocities committed by Belgian colonists. He was knighted in 1911 and, after war-time dealings with Germany in the cause of Irish nationalism, was hanged by the British in 1916. He reappeared in Conrad's life during 1903–4. In a letter to John Quinn, 24 May 1916, Conrad noted: 'For some three weeks he [Casement] lived in the same room in the Matadi Station . . . He knew the coast languages well. I went with him several times on short expeditions to hold "palavers" with neighbouring village-chiefs. The object of them was procuring porters for the company's caravans from Matadi to Leopoldville . . .' (Quoted by Norman Sherry, *Conrad's Western World* [Cambridge: Cambridge University Press, 1971] p. 34).

4. *packing ivory in casks*: Evidence of this activity is to be found in the notebook that contains *The Congo Diary*: a page headed 'Matadi. 23^d.6th.90' contains details of the number of 'pieces' in and the weight of four casks.

5. *Simpson*: James H. Simpson of the Australian ship-owning firm Henry Simpson & Sons, to which the barque *Otago* belonged. Conrad was captain of the *Otago*, his only command, from January 1888 to March 1889.

6. *Gov. B.*: Tadeusz Bobrowski (1824–94), his maternal uncle and guardian.

7. *Purd.*: Identified by Curle as 'Captain Purdy, an acquaintance of Conrad' (*Last Essays* [London: J.M. Dent, 1926], p. 239). Najder could find no trace of a 'Captain Purdy' and suggested, instead, a Glasgow sailor, William Purdu, who served as first mate with Conrad on the *Loch Etive* in 1880. He appears in *The Mirror of the Sea* as P. (*The Mirror of the Sea* [London: J.M. Dent, 1923], pp. 39–45).

8. *Hope*: Conrad's friendship with G.F.W. Hope had begun in 1880. He had served in the *Duke of Sutherland* (though not at the same time as Conrad) and subsequently became a 'Director of Companies' (*HD*, p. 15). Conrad was to go sailing in the *Nellie* with him. (See 'Introduction', p. xxiii).

9. *Cap Froud*: The secretary of the London Ship-Masters' Society. In *A Personal Record*, Conrad writes: 'Dear Captain Froud – it is impossible not to pay him the tribute of affectionate familiarity at this distance of years – had very sound views as to the advancement of knowledge and status for the whole body of the officers of the mercantile marine' (*A Personal Record* [London: J.M. Dent, 1923], p. 7).

10. *Mar.*: Marguerite Poradowska (1848–1937), widow of Conrad's cousin, Aleksander Poradowski, the 'aunt' who helped Conrad obtain his position in the Congo. There is a letter (dated 18 June) sent to her from Matadi (see Frederick Karl and Laurence Davies [eds.] *The Collected Letters of Joseph Conrad*, I [Cambridge: Cambridge University Press, 1983], pp. 56–7). If Conrad wrote to her again on 24 June, the letter has not survived. None of the other letters mentioned here seems to have survived.

11. *speaking ill of each other*: Compare the account of life at the 'Central Station' (*HD*, pp. 45–6).

12. *Mr Harou*: Prosper Harou, a Belgian agent of the Société Anonyme Belge, who arrived from Europe in the same boat as Conrad.

13. *2 Danes in Compny*: Najder notes that many Scandinavians served as officers in the Society's steamboats. See also Norman Sherry, *Conrad's Western World*, pp. 17–91.

14. *Nsoke-River*: Correctly, the Nseke River.

15. *Congo da Lemba*: Stanley refers to this as a place he had known 'some years ago' as 'a flourishing village', but the chief had tried to exact tolls from 'Free State' caravans so the Free State had sent in a force of Bengalas, who had beheaded him and burned down the village (*In Darkest Africa* [London, 1890] p. 82).

16. *market place*: Probably Mazamba. Conrad presumably bought his '1st chicken' there.

17. *the bridge*: The iron bridge over the Lufu River.

18. *Great market*: Probably Nkazura.

19. *Banza Manteka*: Stanley was here on 1 April 1887, when he had visited the missionaries Mr and Mrs Richards at the Livingstone Inland Mission (*In Darkest Africa*, p. 83). In Conrad's time the missionary was Charles E. Ingham, author of *Congo Reading Book*, 2 vols. (London, 1890–91). Conrad has a note 'Banza Manteka – Mr Ingham' at the back of his Congo notebook.

20. *camp^g place*: Probably Tombo Lukuti.

21. *Shot?*: Compare 'Once a white man in an unbuttoned uniform, camping on the path [. . .] was looking after the upkeep of the road, he declared. Can't say I saw any road or any upkeep, unless the body of a middle-aged negro, with a bullet-hole in the forehead, upon which I absolutely stumbled three miles farther on, may be considered as a permanent improvement' (*HD*, p. 39).

22. *Luinzono River*: Correctly, Unionzo River.

23. *Gov^t. Zanzibari with register*: The Congo Free State frequently employed Zanzibaris as soldiers or policemen.

24. *ravines cutting the plain*: Compare the description in *Heart of Darkness*: 'a stamped-in network of paths spreading over the empty land, through long grass, through burnt grass, through thickets, down and up chilly ravines, up and down stony hills ablaze with heat' (*HD*, p. 39).

25. *'malafu'*: Palm wine.

26. *Market place*: Nsekelolo. The market opened daily between 10 and 11 a.m. and closed around 2 p.m.

27. *Mpwe R.*: Correctly, Mpete River.

28. *shouts and drumming in distant villages*: Compare 'Perhaps on some quiet night the tremor of far-off drums, sinking, swelling, a tremor vast, faint; a sound weird, appealing, suggestive, and wild' (*HD*, p. 39).

29. *Manyamba*: Nkonzo Mayamba.

30. *Nsona*: Nsona Kibaka.

31. *market place*: Nkenghe Mwembi.

32. *passed 2 villages*: Probably Wombo, where the old village and the new village were in close proximity.

33. *Inkandu*: Correctly, Nkandu Ndunga.

34. *Route very accidented*: From the French *accidenté* (uneven, rough, hilly). Conrad knew French long before he knew English, and he was, of course, speaking a lot of French in the Congo.

35. *manioc plantations*: The 'stuff like half-cooked dough' (*HD*, p. 70) that Marlow sees the Bangala crew eating was made from the tuberous roots of the manioc.

36. *Messrs Heyn & Jaeger*: Both men were agents of the Société Anonyme Belge. Reginald Heyn, an Englishman, was manager of a transport base at Manyanga.

37. *Stayed here till the 25*: Conrad never fully explained the reason for this protracted stay. For more detailed discussion, see Zdzisław Najder, *Joseph Conrad: A Chronicle* (Cambridge: Cambridge University Press, 1983), pp. 130–31.

38. W. Holman Bentley provides the key to this list. He notes that 'Markets in these parts are held once in every four days; the names of the days being *Nsona, Nkandu, Konzo, Nkenge*' (*Pioneering in the Congo* [London: Religious Tract Society, 1900], I, p. 358). He later clarifies this: 'The Congo week consists of four days ... The markets are named after the day of the week and the town near which they are held' (I. p. 399). Conrad is planning his itinerary for the next two weeks, and he translates the seven days of the European week into the four days of the Congo week, perhaps to calculate when his journey is likely to coincide with market-day. They left Manyanga on the 25th; they reached Nsona Kienzi on the 26th and the Luasi River on the 27th; they passed Nsona Nsungi and the Ngoma River on the 28th; they reached the Inkissi River on the 29th, the Luila River on the 31st and Nselemba on the 1st – a day ahead of schedule. The notebook includes an earlier conversion table, running from 28 June (the day they left Matadi) to 9 July. After listing the four days of the week and describing the system of market-days and place-names, the *Carte des routes de portage* advised 'En quittant Matadi

il faut donc s'informer du jour de la semaine fiote auquel on est
arrivé.'

39. *Market place*: Probably Nsona Kienzi, and, therefore, probably
market-day. (According to the itinerary provided for Belgian State Officials, markets would not necessarily take place every four days: some
might be on an eight-day [i.e. two-week] cycle.)

40. *Mrs Comber*: Mrs Comber (née Annie Smith) had only recently
arrived at the mission, and she would be dead before Conrad returned to
Europe. She had come out from England earlier in the year and had
married Percy Comber, an English Baptist missionary, at Matadi in
June. She died at Banana on 19 December 1890 after repeated fevers,
while waiting for a home-going steamer. A photograph of her is included
in W. Holman Bentley's *Pioneering in the Congo*, II, p. 166. Percy
Comber had arrived in the Congo in 1885, and he died there of fever in
January 1892.

41. *Mr Davis Miss*: Philip Davies, another Baptist missionary, arrived in
the Congo with Percy Comber in 1885. From October 1886 he was
stationed at Wathen, where he died in December 1895. His photograph
appears in Bentley, II, p. 359.

42. *Rev. Bentley*: Rev. W. Holman Bentley, author of *Pioneering in the
Congo*. (See 'Introduction', p. xxiii.) Bentley and his wife had gone to
Tungwa, near Makuta (Bentley, II, p. 341).

43. *much more trees*: Najder notes this as a Polonism (*wiele więcej drzew*).

44. *Nzungi*: Nsona Nsungi, village and market, but this was not market-
day.

45. *a very decent bridge*: Near Nkonzo Mbimbi.

46. *One wrecked*: The *Florida* was wrecked on 18 July, but was refloated
and brought back to Kinshasa in five days (Sherry, p. 41). Compare:
'One of them [. . .] informed me with great volubility and many digressions
[. . .] that my steamer was at the bottom of the river' (*HD*, p. 40).

47. *shimbek*: African word for a few huts occupied by people of the same
employment (e.g., railway builders).

48. *Ipeca*: Ipecacuanha, a herbal medicine used for dysentery.

49. *Row with carriers all the way*: Compare: 'Then he got fever, and had
to be carried in a hammock slung under a pole. As he weighed sixteen
stone I had no end of rows with the carriers' (*HD*, p. 40).

50. *made a speech which they did not understand*: Compare: 'one evening, I
made a speech in English with gestures, not one of which was lost to the
sixty pairs of eyes before me' (*HD*, p. 40).

READ MORE IN PENGUIN

In every corner of the world, on every subject under the sun, Penguin represents quality and variety – the very best in publishing today.

For complete information about books available from Penguin – including Puffins, Penguin Classics and Arkana – and how to order them, write to us at the appropriate address below. Please note that for copyright reasons the selection of books varies from country to country.

In the United Kingdom: Please write to *Dept. EP, Penguin Books Ltd, Bath Road, Harmondsworth, West Drayton, Middlesex UB7 0DA*

In the United States: Please write to *Consumer Services, Penguin Putnam Inc., 405 Murray Hill Parkway, East Rutherford, New Jersey 07073-2136.* VISA and MasterCard holders call 1-800-631-8571 to order Penguin titles

In Canada: Please write to *Penguin Books Canada Ltd, 10 Alcorn Avenue, Suite 300, Toronto, Ontario M4V 3B2*

In Australia: Please write to *Penguin Books Australia Ltd, 487 Maroondah Highway, Ringwood, Victoria 3134*

In New Zealand: Please write to *Penguin Books (NZ) Ltd, Private Bag 102902, North Shore Mail Centre, Auckland 10*

In India: Please write to *Penguin Books India Pvt Ltd, 11 Community Centre, Panchsheel Park, New Delhi 110017*

In the Netherlands: Please write to *Penguin Books Netherlands bv, Postbus 3507, NL-1001 AH Amsterdam*

In Germany: Please write to *Penguin Books Deutschland GmbH, Metzlerstrasse 26, 60594 Frankfurt am Main*

In Spain: Please write to *Penguin Books S. A., Bravo Murillo 19, 1°B, 28015 Madrid*

In Italy: Please write to *Penguin Italia s.r.l., Via Vittorio Emanuele 45ia, 20094 Corsico, Milano*

In France: Please write to *Penguin France, 12, Rue Prosper Ferradou, 31700 Blagnac*

In Japan: Please write to *Penguin Books Japan Ltd, Iidabashi KM-Bldg, 2-23-9 Koraku, Bunkyo-Ku, Tokyo 112-0004*

In South Africa: Please write to *Penguin Books South Africa (Pty) Ltd, P.O. Box 751093, Gardenview, 2047 Johannesburg*

BY THE SAME AUTHOR

'Conrad is among the very greatest novelists in the language – or any language' F. R. Leavis, *The Great Tradition*

A Personal Record *and* **The Mirror of the Sea**
With a new introduction and notes by Mara Kalnins

Conrad is a largely enigmatic presence in his novels, but in *A Personal Record* (1908–1909) he decided to introduce his readers to 'the figure behind the veil'. Almost equally revealing is *The Mirror of the Sea* (1904–6), written 'in tribute to the sea, its ships, and its men, to whom I remain indebted for so much which has gone to make me what I am'.

Lord Jim

The novel by which Conrad is most often remembered by perhaps a majority of readers, and the first considerable novel he wrote.

Under Western Eyes

An atmosphere of ominous suspense hangs over this story of revolutionaries, set in Switzerland and Russia.

Nostromo

His story of revolution in South America, which Arnold Bennett regarded 'as one of the greatest novels of any age'.

also published:

Almayer's Folly	**Tales of Unrest**
An Outcast of the Islands	**'Twixt Land and Sea**
Chance	**Typhoon and Other Stories**
The Nigger of the 'Narcissus'	**Victory**
The Rescue	**Within the Tides**
The Secret Agent	**Youth** *and* **The End of the Tether**
The Shadow-Line	

Heart of Darkness, read by David Threlfall, *Victory: An Island Tale* and *Nostromo*, both read by Michael Pennington, are all available as Penguin Audiobooks.